"This is more than a book, it's a ministry in print. It gets to the heart of the matter, touching areas that the church has long covered up or overlooked. Now Black Christian singles have a helpmate!"

Jerry Adkisson
Singles Ministry President
The Temple Church, Nashville, Tennessee

"Dr. Chris Jackson gives us a fresh and creative approach to the standards, hopes, and possibilities for Christians who are single. He challenges singles to seek wholeness and fulfillment in Christ. It is a very good book."

Dr. John H. Corbitt
National Dean
National Baptist Congress of Christian Education
Greenville, South Carolina

"Chris Jackson's very unique seminar on relationships is presented each semester in my Human Sexuality classes. Student response is overwhelming, which accounts for his widespread popularity as a speaker."

Professor Gloria Lewis
Psychology Department
Tennessee State University

Also by Chris Jackson

Straight Talk on Tough Topics

The Black Christian Singles Guide To

DATING AND SEXUALITY

Chris Jackson

GRAND RAPIDS, MICHIGAN 49530

ZONDERVAN™

The Black Christian Singles Guide to Dating and Sexuality
Copyright © 1999 by Chris Jackson

Requests for information should be addressed to:

Zondervan, *Grand Rapids, Michigan 49530*

Library of Congress Cataloging-in-Publication Data

Jackson, Chris.
    The Black Christian singles guide to dating and sexuality / Chris Jackson.
      p. cm.
    Includes bibliographical references (p.).
    ISBN 0-310-22344-X (softcover)
      1. Afro-American single people—Religious life. 2. Dating (Social customs)—
Religious aspects—Christianity. 3. Sex—Religious aspects—Christianity. I. Title.
BV4596.S5 J33 1998
    241'.66'08996073—ddc21   98-37490

Interior design by Pamela Eicher

Printed in the United States of America

01 02 03 04 05 06 /❖ DC/ 10 9 8 7 6 5

This book is dedicated to every single who has ever had sincere-but-unanswered questions about the single state.

CONTENTS

PREFACE

- Have you ever lain in bed at night after watching too much late-night TV and found yourself wide-eyed and staring at the ceiling with every fiber of your body and aching for the comfort and companionship of a serious soul mate?
- Have you ever lain in bed with a partner and, in spite of the sensational sex, you feel unexplainedly empty and strongly unfulfilled?
- Perhaps you are currently in a perfect "4.0" relationship with the man or woman of your dreams but you are wondering if your love has enough stamina to last through the major league marathon of a lifelong marriage.

So many questions and seemingly so few answers—until now. This book was written from the crucial vantage point of an African-American male who was single until he was thirty-eight years old. It is my privilege to serve you this meal fresh from the kitchen of my experiences combined with the recipes of my research on the subject. It is drenched in the joys and simmered in the solitude that uniquely comes from a life of living single. To use a different metaphor, sometimes the single life can seem like a high-tech roller coaster with a series of thrilling highs, depressing lows, and a variety of unexpected twists and turns along the way. Singleness, like most other conditions in life, has its advantages and disadvantages. And like a passenger on a roller coaster, you can complain about the wind in your face, or you can sit back and enjoy the ride.

I hope that this book upsets you in places. I also hope it makes you laugh, cry, and nod your head affirmatively. Usually significant alterations are made in the fabric of our lives only when we feel strongly about something. Emotions tend to move us to action. Regardless of the many emotions encountered as you read, my greatest desire is that this book would cause you to think and to grow.

You may not agree with each viewpoint, but hopefully each point will at least provoke individual thought and stimulate group discussion. Too often we adopt the easy route of accepting the opinions of the majority rather than taking the time and energy necessary to forge our own personal perspective. Finally, may you personally grow in many areas of your life through reading this book as much as I have grown through the process of researching and writing it.

ACKNOWLEDGMENTS

Appreciation is expressed to the following people and groups who have directly and indirectly contributed in small and great ways to the successful development of this book:

To God Almighty: Thank you for your love, guidance, power, and inspiration, which all enable me to fulfill my purpose in life

To my parents, Andrew and Christine Jackson, and my extended family: I honor you for providing an example, an education, and encouragement and for instilling in me a sense of entrepreneurship

To my wife, Coreen, and sons Joshua, Juleon, and Jemiah: Thank you for your love, support, and book suggestions and for believing in me

To my office administrator, Chandra Allen: Thanks for your patience, persistence, and professionalism demonstrated in producing the initial printed manuscript

To my students—the Baptist Student Union groups from Tennessee State University and Fisk University: You have my heart and have been a great inspiration for this book

To my pastor and first lady, Michael Lee Graves and Eleanor Graves: Thanks for your positive example and for encouraging me to pursue excellence in life and ministry

To the Temple Singles Ministry: Thanks for your input to the questions in this book and for allowing me to test some of this material on you first

To the Missouri Black Christian Singles Conference: Thanks for my foundation in singles ministry and for demonstrating excellence in this very important field of work

To the Tennessee Baptist Convention and the Nashville Baptist Association: Thanks for allowing me to develop my gifts and to explore ministry areas beyond the immediate focus

To the national B.S.U. Retreat: It is always a joy and never a chore to work with such a hungry and exciting group as you

To Dr. John H. Corbitt and the National Baptist Congress Workshop: I have always said you are the cream of the crop. So keep on climbing and don't ever stop

To my editor, Jim Ruark: Thanks for your careful work with me and for looking below the surface of sensitive subject matter in order to grasp my true intentions. You understood my heart's motive of enlightening the minds, encouraging the lives, and empowering the spirits of singles

To my publisher, Zondervan: Thanks for trusting me with this book and for making it available to so many people for the glory of God

Chapter 1

SINGLENESS: BURDEN, BLESSING, OR BOTH?

The Challenges and Rewards of Being Single

A lthough various inner struggles can accompany singleness, a much greater battle is often waged against society's warped perception of singles. There is a general lack of acceptance of singles in a society that caters to couples. In spite of Americans' remaining single longer, and despite the fact that a large percentage of the African-American population is single, stereotypical impressions still abound. Let us examine three common misconceptions about singles.

MYTH #1: "IF YOU'RE SINGLE YOU MUST BE SAD"

One perspective supposes that a single person could not possibly be experiencing all the joys and thrills that life holds for a married person. Although it is true that even the simple joys of life can potentially be multiplied through matrimony, this is certainly not guaranteed. The image of the sad single is so pervasive that many singles who have a weak sense of self-worth tend to go from relationship to relationship without a rest simply because they must be with someone—anyone— in order to feel validated. Sometimes this is a subconscious reaction, and it may unfortunately take a lifetime to admit and correct such counterproductive behavior.

To avoid the trap of the "Sad Single," we must seek a dependable source of validation. This source cannot be *external validation*. External validation seeks personal props from the outside for us to remain sane. When respected people approve of, give compliments to, flatter, flirt with, or otherwise stroke the ego of such a single, everything is lovely. Of course, everyone needs to be needed by others from time to time, but if being liked by others becomes a priority, we are headed for a lifetime of disappointment. People can be unpredictable. Once we think we have figured out how they want us to act and we conform our behavior accordingly, they change their minds. If a person adopts this pattern of conformity for an extended amount of time, this behavior could result in a mild-to-serious case of schizophrenia. The requirements of external validation are hardly worth the rewards—especially when we consider the alternatives.

One positive alternative is *internal validation.* This phrase refers to seeking value and worth from inside ourselves. We are created in the image of God and are packed with such valuable elements as a mind to think about the present, a memory to reflect upon the past, and an imagination to dream about the future. We are wealthy if we possess a conscience, a talent, or a gift to share with the rest of creation. Many of the answers to the puzzles of life lie locked inside us as we busily embark upon repeated attempts to discover truth and meaning. This current "drive-through" culture is a rapid world of "get there in a hurry, do it quicker, send it sooner and get it faster." We have instant everything but we need to learn how to STOP . . . and be quiet for a change. Your inner voice desires an appointment with you. If we listen, we can learn a lot from someone who can very easily become an intimate stranger: our inner self.

A third source of validation is *eternal validation,* which can also be very near or very far, depending on our desire. This level of validation is important because it will remain even during those days when our external support system is dysfunctional and our internal flame has begun to flicker. Eternal validation does not rely on the unpredictable fickleness of other people or the unintentional human shortcomings within ourselves. This type of validation depends on a source and a force far greater than could ever be exhausted by worldly means. Eternal validation is a phenomenon that extends beyond family, race, or mere religion. It refers to a personal relationship with a powerful God who desires to take us beyond our heritage and traditions so that we can discover our ultimate God-given purpose in life. The person who knows his or her purpose is destined to make a difference. We will examine this in detail in chapter 12. Right now let's look at the second singles stereotype.

MYTH #2: "IF YOU'RE SINGLE YOU MUST BE SEARCHING"

How many times have well-meaning people attempted to "hook you up" with some other equally unsuspecting single? Usually the reaction is nervous laughter, perhaps a shy grin, or maybe even a muttered or unspoken "why don't they just leave me alone?" This scenario is particularly prevalent for singles who actually seem content with their singleness. And when this contentedness is coupled with age, "God's little helpers" seem to appear in droves. There is an unspoken assumption on the part of humanity-at-large that all singles are constantly on the lookout for a mate or anything closely resembling such a relationship.

Many movies and television shows reinforce this mind-set. Although such media may depict real-life situations, it must be understood that not all singles desire to dangle themselves as mate-bait. Many singles have lived long enough and have been through enough stuff to know that the company of an empty head is much worse than an empty bed. It is better to be emotionally unattached than to be relationally mismatched. This leads us to our third category of singles.

MYTH #3: "IF YOU'RE SINGLE YOU MUST BE GAY"

Now it's testimony time. I was invited to speak at a church as part of an anniversary program. A few days after the invitation was given, it was courteously withdrawn, without explanation. After a little investigation, I discovered that the only reason I was disinvited was that the pastor of the church frowned upon my being "over 30 and not married." The clear implication was that I might be gay. That was it: My actions, mannerisms, behavior, and morals were never in question. But that didn't seem to matter.

While this incident was—one hopes—an extreme case, it is indicative of what many people speculate but few verbalize. This stereotype is even held by some singles, especially on a date when a woman is sexually reserved or when a man fails to grab at anything that attracts him. Two things apply in such cases: (1) Not all persons are designed or destined to be married or even coupled. If this is their choice—whether temporarily or permanently—leave them alone! We cannot force people into a preconceived social script for their lives. This is particularly true when that script is validated by God and not harmful to others. (2) If you are on a date with someone who is kind and respectful but does not indicate a burning desire to jump in the backseat of the car at the next stoplight, don't panic. This does not necessarily mean that your date is homosexual. Indeed, sexual pressure has spoiled many relationships because the expression was rushed and therefore premature. We will address this problem further in chapters 3 and 4.

PRIVILEGES AND RESPONSIBILITIES OF SINGLES

Almost every stage in life has its positives and negatives. The advantages of childhood lie in its carefree nature, with all the necessities provided by someone else; however, the *privileges* of childhood are also limited. The advantages of adulthood lie in the achievement of goals; yet, there are all the *responsibilities* that go along with this stage. Senior adulthood may provide the luxury of retirement and travel, but physical bodies are usually not as strong and lithe as they used to be and therefore the rate and scope of activity are limited.

If we develop the attitude of focusing only on the negatives, we could actually be depressed for a lifetime. However, if we choose to accentuate the positives, we can accept and enjoy life and the rich variety of its stages. The key is contentment coupled with a positive attitude. Now let us apply the same principles to the phenomenon of singleness. Far too many singles choose to have the blues when it comes to their station in life rather than making the choice to rejoice. This happens usually because there is an unconscious decision to focus on the flaws of life rather than appreciating the advantages. Let me suggest five possible advantages and disadvantages of singleness.

DISADVANTAGES	ADVANTAGES
1. Lack of regular companionship	1. Opportunity for vigorous self-development
2. Childlessness	2. Opportunity to share more time, talent, and resources with others
3. Absence of a fulfilling sexual relationship	3. Opportunity to honor God with service and to prepare for the future
4. Fewer social invitations than couples	4. Opportunity to design custom-made events for yourself or with other singles
5. Feelings of unconnectedness and detachment	5. Opportunity to come and go at will without elaborate reconfiguration of schedules

In comparing these lists we can see that for every obstacle there is an opportunity; for every perceived problem there is also a privilege. So much of life depends on which perception we choose to use. In his helpful book *For Singles Only*, Robyn Gool warns against marriage as a "quick fix" for personal problems. He states,

> Even the happiest of married people experience occasional feelings of loneliness. That's just part of being human. The answer is not constant human companionship as much as it is continual fellowship with God. The only true solution to human loneliness is a closer walk with the Creator.[1]

Joni Eareckson Tada is a speaker, singer, painter, and quadriplegic. Although now married, she wrote the following words of wisdom while she was single:

> Acceptance of the role of being single ends the frustration of not knowing. But that's the hardest part. Surrender to the idea of being forever single, with all the sacrifices that implies, is the most difficult. But once acceptance is made, living with that role is easier. This is not to say God will never allow us to

marry someday. Maybe He will; maybe He won't. What I'm saying is that it doesn't matter because we leave the choice and decision with Him. We trust His judgment that all things work together for our good if we love God. Only God is capable of telling us what our rights and needs are. You have to surrender that right to Him. Begin your life as a single person, working and living according to the priorities of serving and glorifying Him. In turn, God gives a rich and satisfying life. In place of one partner, He brings many friends into our lives to meet our emotional needs and loneliness.[2]

SIX STUMBLING BLOCKS OF SINGLENESS

The single state of life poses some specific challenges. Of course, not every item mentioned will apply to every reader at present, but it may apply in the future to you or a friend.

SEPARATION FROM PARENTS

At first glance, separation from parents may not seem to be a potentially troublesome condition. Many people make a very smooth transition in leaving home. However, for others the cutting of the proverbial parental apron strings is arduous and accompanied by much pain and frustration. Several factors come into play in this process:

- How close was your relationship with your parents while you were growing up?
- What was the relationship like between your parents as husband and wife?
- Did your parents shelter, cling to, or strongly depend on you?
- Especially if you're a man, was there a wholesome father figure in the home?
- Were you exposed to a variety of social situations, and did you spend adequate time with friends outside the home?

Answers to these and other questions can help us assess the relative degree of difficulty experienced in the process of achieving independence. Expressing the need to separate from parents does not imply disrespect, dishonor, or disregard in any sense. Strong family links are needed for as long as there is life. However, successful development as single adults must involve independence and self-reliance.

I can remember parting with my parents the day after my graduation from college. I was headed to New York to do mission work for the summer. Until then, Dad had always made it a point to slip me a little cash whenever I was headed out of town. That morning as we stood in the busy airport hallway and said our final good-byes, I waited for the customary "Here's a little something for your trip." Instead, he simply said, "Have a nice trip." As I turned and walked toward my plane, with every stride I began to experience new feelings of instantaneous maturity. Although it was a strange sensation, it was unexplainedly a welcomed wake-up call to the reality of my newfound independence. It roused me from my carefree world of parental provision and clearly alerted me to my need to begin to fend for myself. It was such a small act—but I appreciated it.

Although sometimes parents admittedly hold too tightly to the parent-child relationship, at other times it is the single who perpetuates the overdependence. Reasons for this may range from psychological dependency to immaturity to just plain laziness. A major step in achieving independence is to move physically out of your parents' home. This usually sends a strong message to both the parents and the single that something has changed. This message can be undergirded through inviting the parents over for dinner after getting firmly established. Such an experience can provide a tremendous sense of accomplishment for the parents as well as for the single.

SELFISHNESS

Few people desire to be known as selfish or self-centered, but the fact is that some singles fit squarely into this category. When living alone, it is easy to slip into a "me mode" of thinking and acting. Singles do not have to consult with anyone as to the color scheme of the bathroom, the music for the afternoon, or the menu for the week. No one has to agree to the purchases made, friends chosen, or trips planned. If they are not careful, singles can unintentionally grow to believe that the world revolves around them. Here are some of the symptoms of such a mind-set:

- Expressing dissatisfaction whenever things don't go your way
- Failing to consider the desires and opinions of others when making plans
- Being unable to rejoice when someone else is blessed even when it does not involve you
- Being a poor listener, or tending to make conversation continually revolve around yourself and your concerns
- Spending much money on self but seldom spending it on others

One way to begin breaking out of self-centeredness is to consciously start acting the opposite of the behaviors suggested above. It has been said that a person wrapped up in self makes too small a package to serve as a good gift. One of life's strange paradoxes is that the more we give to others, the more we ourselves receive.

SPENDING

Financial spending is closely linked to selfishness, and it can be crippling. Unnecessary debt can easily and gradually accumulate in our lives so that by the time we realize our mistake, the damage is already done. The so-called American Dream can quickly become the American Nightmare if we do not give extreme care to the control and discipline of our finances. Consider the not-too-subtle exploitation in television advertisements and the unspoken peer pressure to purchase the latest fashions, gadgets, or transportation, American society places very little emphasis on restraint. The messages we experience on any given day range from "Just do it" to "Obey your thirst." The media and the culture promote propaganda that essentially reasons: "You work hard, you deserve this, life is short, so go for it because you only go around once." All this sounds sane on the surface, but what they *don't* tell you is that although life is short, their interest rate is high; and *you* may only go around once, but their *bill* comes every month. Mature singles come to the point of realizing the following simple life principles:

- Just because I see it and like it does not mean I need it.
- I must practice deferred gratification: putting off the immediate desires of today in order to obtain the greater goals of tomorrow.
- I must never allow my financial outgo to exceed my financial income.

- I must invest in myself through saving or investing at least 10 percent of every paycheck.
- I must learn the principle of sowing and reaping through tithing and sharing with others.

One of the best investments you can make as a single is buying a home. Too many African-Americans unfortunately direct their purchasing power primarily toward goods and services that depreciate in value: clothes, cars, food, entertainment, and beauty care. Property is usually a very solid investment because it will always be in demand and typically increases in value over time. Get out of that rented apartment and invest in yourself rather than in your landlord.

I purchased my first home as a single person shortly after completing grad school. Buying that first house was scary, but I knew that I did not want to spend the rest of my life renting. Buying a house helped me to build homeowner equity and also helped greatly at tax time. I stayed in the house eight years and could have had it almost paid in full had I known then what I know now about owning property. (See "Six Mortgage 'Secrets' That Can Save You Money" on the next page.)

One of the greatest financial enemies of singles, couples, or any undisciplined human being is the deliciously deceptive phenomenon of credit cards. A friend of mine amassed a personal debt of $60,000 during four years of college—much of that as a result of the easy and seemingly painless process of saying, "Charge it." That person, Pastor Amos Howard, has since emerged from debt and now leads dynamic Debt-Free seminars nationwide. Apart from obtaining a reasonable car and house that fit your budget, personal debt is a noose around your neck that you don't need if you expect to live and breathe normally. If you are currently in significant debt, stop now, cut up those credit cards, and commit yourself to paying off those bills before you incur new ones. This may require some sacrifice now, but you will love yourself for it later.

STRESS

Sometimes singles manage to acquire a level of stress that surpasses that of the rest of the population. Consider some of the reasons why singles develop stress:

SIX MORTGAGE "SECRETS" THAT CAN SAVE YOU MONEY

These simple tips can literally save you thousands of dollars and move you more quickly down the road to financial independence.

1. The thirty-year-loan is usually a poor choice for the home buyer. The interest over that length of time will cause you to pay significantly beyond the original price. Seek a fifteen-year loan.[3]

2. If possible, make an additional principle payment on the day your loan is activated. This simple action will shave time and thousands of dollars off the duration and amount of your loan.

3. Ask your lender for an "amortization schedule" and include an extra principle payment above the stated amount on each mortgage payment.

4. Make a partial payment every two weeks. This tactic is similar in effect to no. 2 and will drastically reduce the length and amount of your loan because you will be making one extra payment per year.[4]

5. Shop around for the lowest interest rate and the lowest "points" available.

6. Do not hesitate to haggle with the lender or the seller about anything you want to change about the deal. If you are refinancing an FHA loan, try to close near the end of the month to avoid duplicating interest payments. Remember at all times that it is you who control the flow of money, not the mortgage institution.

- Overcommitment—a problem exacerbated by the expectations of married people who think that because you are single you have all the time in the world.
- Misplaced priorities
- Failure to plan
- Procrastination

Other stress producers stem from ordinary life experiences ranging from something as serious as a personal or family illness, to something seemingly as simple as changing a job or a residence. Stress can cause breakdowns in communication and relationships. It may show up through job-career ineffectiveness. Sometimes stress may also have a spiritual foundation. The Mental Health Association of the Ozarks has developed a three-step plan to combat stress that essentially states:

1. *Welcome challenges:* Realize that life is a process. Stay open to learning, and don't be afraid of new people and new experiences.
2. *Develop control:* Create your own happiness and learn to build on your strengths.
3. *Commit to your purpose:* Discover your central purpose in life, work toward it, and give it your very best.

Because singles may not always have an immediate support system, it is sometimes easy to become discouraged. When this occurs, you may need to try one or more of the following suggestions to pull yourself out of depression or discouragement:

- Try not to exaggerate.
- Decide not to whine.
- Make sure you are well rested.
- Consider whether you need to repent.
- Consider whether you need to rejoice.
- Consider whether you need to forgive.
- Consider whether you need to take some action.
- Consider whether you need to trust God more.

Remember that life has too much to offer to shortchange yourself and others through depression and discouragement.

SEXUAL PITFALLS

We can fall into a variety of unhealthy sexual situations sometimes set up by others. These pitfalls tend to be well camouflaged and therefore very easy to miss except for a discerning eye. This book details these aspects of sexuality in chapters 5 and 6.

SPIRITUAL IMBALANCE

Perhaps one of the most overlooked reasons that some singles stumble is spiritual imbalance. As human beings we were created with a need to know, love, and honor God. This genuine need has been replaced, however, with counterfeits in the form of relationships, careers, possessions, chemicals, and an assortment of other "fake fillers." The sad reality is that no matter how long and how hard we may search for a way to fill the void we were born with, nothing will ever fill it except a personal relationship with God.

You may feel that you have tried almost everything, but you still remain dissatisfied. Perhaps you have placed your heart in the hand of a man or a woman only to have that person carelessly drop it and shatter it. Or maybe you don't know exactly what the problem is but you know you have no peace inside, there is something missing, and there must be more to life. If this reflects the way you feel, please allow me to invite you to pray this simple prayer:

> Dear God, I need you. I believe that you love me and that you have something special for me to be and to do. I realize that I have not been what you created me to be because I have been trying to live life in my own power. I now relinquish my control and gladly surrender to your control. Jesus, I believe that you died on the cross for me, and I now accept your love, forgiveness, and power for my life by faith. Thank you, Lord, for coming inside of me right now. Amen.

If you sincerely prayed this prayer, then the God of the universe just entered your life by faith. This is not the end but only the beginning of an exciting and abundant life of faith. Please be sure to take these important next steps:

- Daily devour and obey the promises and instructions of the Bible.
- Daily communicate with God through prayer.
- Get in constant companionship with strong, godly people who will help you to grow.
- Begin to share your faith with others and discover and use your spiritual gifts.

As a single you have the unique opportunity to develop a deep and undistracted devotion to God. Don't waste this precious privilege but, rather, give God's rulership and character first priority in your life. When you do that, all the other concerns of life will tend to fall into place (Matthew 6:33).

LET'S TALK!

1. How does Philippians 4:11–13 relate to the subject of singleness?
2. Do you consider *your* singleness to be a burden, a blessing, or both? Explain.
3. What do you like least about being single?
4. What do you like most about being single?
5. To which of the three myths about singleness can you most closely relate? Explain.
6. How would you describe your relationship with your parents? Has the relationship been a help or a hindrance to your singleness?
7. Do you consider yourself a selfish person? Do you know other singles who are self-centered? Discuss possible causes and cures for selfishness among singles.
8. How many credit cards do you possess? How many credit cards do you need? Do you have debt beyond your car loan, mortgage, and basic living expenses? What is your plan to reduce your debt? What are some ways that debt could negatively affect and influence many other aspects of life? Do you currently own your own home, and if not, why not?
9. What usually causes stress in your life? What usually relieves stress in your life?
10. What are some potential sexual pitfalls for singles? How can singles become more aware of potential sex traps?
11. What are some symptoms of spiritual imbalance? What are some solutions for spiritual imbalance?

Chapter 2

MALE AND FEMALE: APPRECIATING THE DIFFERENCES

Making the Contrasts Work for You, Not Against You

For several years now I have refused to use the term *opposite sex* because of the negative psychological connotation of the phrase. I have observed too many marriages and other male-female relationships in which the two who are supposed to be allies act more like enemies. Rather than building each other up, they specialize in tearing each other down. Since the word *opposite* means "to oppose,"[1] the term *opposite sex* fosters division rather than the cooperation we need to see.

I have discovered, however, that there are positive as well as negative definitions for the word *opposition.* We usually associate this word with such terms as *contrary, conflict,* and *combatant.* But other meanings could include *contrast, counterbalance,* and *complement.*

This irony speaks to an important truth about male-female relationships: Every relationship has the capacity to generate life or manufacture death. Every couple should constantly choose to tolerate chaos or to cultivate cooperation. The very health and survival of a relationship has much to do with this decision. No normal person would desire an intimate long-term relationship with someone who was contrary, combatant, and continually in conflict. This sounds like the description of an enemy. How much better it would be to share an intimate relationship with a friend who offers a unique contrast in order to complement and counterbalance our particular personality. Now that's a relationship!

But beware—this kind of real relationship also requires real work. It will never happen automatically. If it occurs at all, it will be intentional.

In a healthy, well-rounded relationship there may be many differences between the two, but the wise couple uses these differences to strengthen the bond rather than weaken it. There is actually a kind of dullness in sameness, but great value in relationship variety. Consider this principle, as illustrated below:

50————————O————————50

Ideas, interests, talents, gifts, experiences, thoughts, perspectives

MAN   WOMAN

The man and woman in the relationship may view life from totally different perspectives. However, a different perspective is not necessarily a wrong one. What if both parties thought, acted, reasoned, and performed exactly alike in most situations?

What a waste of creativity and what a duplication of energy and ability. A couple with a wide array of perspectives can create a more powerful force than a couple with very similar abilities. The key lies in successfully harnessing this variety and both persons must pull together in the same direction. A piano would be boring if it had only major keys or only minor keys. The true beauty and capability of a piano emerges only as the keys are combined to produce a marvelous and harmonic melody through the cooperation of different notes. Distasteful discord occurs when piano chords clash. But when this happens, the fault lies not with the keys themselves or even with the creator of the musical score. Musical beauty is dependent on the skill, practice, ability, and technique of the player.

Before turning our attention to specific differences between males and females, perhaps it would help to examine some other reasons for the high levels of hostility occasionally observed between men and women in general, and between Black men and women in particular. I see two main sources of male-female relationship concept development.

PARENTAL INFLUENCE

The earliest and most powerful shapers of perceptions between the two sexes stem from the closest example observed while growing as a child. This example is usually the parent or guardian. Unfortunately, within the Black community there are three "relationship predators" lurking across the landscape and devouring unprotected couples and families. These predators are commonly known as unwed pregnancy, divorce, and dysfunctional or absentee fathers. A silent scream for help emerges daily from the neighborhood in anguish over the carnage left behind by these merciless menaces to society. These three creatures have left deep, permanent emotional and relational scars across the faces of many singles who experience a grim reminder of their home-life whenever they look into their companion's eyes. It is sometimes difficult to forget traumatic childhood experiences. It can be an exhausting exercise to locate, erase, and rerecord the old mental tapes that we seem to play continuously.

It is hard for someone to exhibit healthy relationship actions and attitudes without ever seeing them modeled in the home. This is why singles owe it to themselves, to the community, and to God to make a heartfelt decision not to contribute further to the frightful statistics regarding unwed pregnancy, divorce, and absentee fatherhood. In more than twenty years of ministry on the college campus and more than twelve years of work with the penal system, I have found that many of the issues I encounter are directly traceable to family problems.

Singleness is the perfect time to begin discovering and recovering from the hurts of our past so that we can continue our lives without the encumbrance of excess emotional weights. An additional incentive is that if you should enter a permanent relationship in the future, you will not have to bring into it unnecessary negative baggage that could hinder your progress and clutter your new life together. There may be a history in your family of divorce, alcohol or drug abuse, pregnancy out of wedlock, crime, depression, absentee fathers, or another emotionally disabling condition. Don't ignore it or run from it; face it and fight it. This may be a sign of a genera-

tional curse that must be broken, corrected, and turned into a blessing. Expunging negative patterns and memories from our lives may
be a painful process, but recovery and healing are definitely worth the
effort and are achievable through counseling, prayer, fasting, and
strong faith and determination.

SOCIAL AND MEDIA INFLUENCE

After the family, the next greatest influence on relationships is that
of media and society. These two can be discussed together because they
so often tend to influence each other. People tend to imitate what they
see on television and hear on the radio; in the same way, television and
radio tend to copy whatever is popular in society. Nothing seems considered off-limits anymore as long as it will sell more music and movies.
One look at B.E.T. *Video Soul* or *Rap City* will reveal more flesh than
one is liable to see at Freaknik. The attitude toward male-female relationships reflected in most contemporary R & B, Rap, Hip Hop, and
New Jack Swing music is strictly a business matter of supply and
demand: The women demand the money and the men had better supply; the men demand the body and the women had better supply.
(Sometimes for variety's sake this pattern is reversed, with the men
demanding the money and the women demanding the body.) A constant entertainment diet of unhealthy words and images has a damaging impact on positive and progressive relationships. If a man only
thinks of a woman as a commodity, or she him, there is no reason to
develop such essential relationship qualities as trust, respect, commitment, and open communication. In the New Jack relationship style, if
my current commodity gives me trouble or becomes a bore, I'll simply
trade that one in or give it to a friend.

We must begin to move toward overcoming "objectification," as
Gary R. Brooks puts it in his book *The Centerfold Syndrome.*[2] We are so
much more than flesh objects. We must begin to give the sublime gift
of respect to ourselves as well as to each other. When we begin to
respect each other and protect each other, we will be much less likely
to suspect each other and reject each other.

SECURITY CHECK

Let us now consider why some relationships work and others get wrecked. In doing so, let us turn to an analogy of airport security. Every modern airport is equipped with an electronic security device that scans carry-on items before we board our plane. The reason for the high-tech precautions is that in years past passengers began transporting unlawful materials or smuggling weapons that could endanger lives. Thirty thousand feet above ground is not a good place to have a crisis, so elaborate measures are in force in an effort to avert a tragedy.

Of course, it would not make much sense to check the passengers and bags *after* takeoff. Yet this is exactly what happens in many marriages and other relationships. Many singles begin asking significant questions about their partners long after "taking off." This may account for the many "surprised singles" who thought they began their relationship flight with one kind of partner only to find themselves skyjacked in midair.

What if all singles were required to pass through a specially equipped and sensitive security check station before entering a new relationship? Consider the various ways one might fail the test.

A. Excess Baggage Impounded

1. A trunk full of unforgiveness and unresolved anger toward parents
   Relationship danger: There is a tendency to "transfer" to our adulthood much of the unfinished emotional business from childhood.
2. A duffel bag full of pain from past relationships
   Relationship danger: Battle wounds from the past can produce distrust, unwarranted comparisons, and fear of future intimacy. Symptoms may include excessive coldness or tendencies toward revenge whenever offended.
3. A suitcase full of codependency and controlling habits
   Relationship danger: Codependency and control can produce some unhealthy habits in the relationship: (1) the "Rescue

Mission" need to be overly needed, and (2) the "Boss Position" need to be always top seeded.

B. Unlawful Weapons Confiscated

1. A dagger of dishonesty
    Relationship danger: Dishonesty threatens the trust that lies at the very heart of every good relationship.
2. A pistol of possessiveness along with a 9mm revolver of pride
    Relationship danger: Possessiveness suffocates a couple's sense of freedom, and pride prevents two very important words: "I'm sorry."
3. Explosives of repressed resentment
    Relationship danger: Bottled-up feelings are eventually uncapped, and this usually occurs at inappropriate times and in inappropriate ways.

C. Illegal Substances Discovered

1. A case of chronic criticism
    Relationship danger: Constant criticism wears on the ability of the criticized person to be loved and accepted for who he or she is rather than because he or she fits into a prescribed proper pattern of behavior.
2. A kilo of coldness and emotional distance
    Relationship danger: Every time we emotionally pull away from our partner we create what Gary Smalley describes as a "mini-divorce."[3] Too many emotional icicles in a relationship eventually produce an emotional iceberg.
3. A dime bag of self-centeredness
    Relationship danger: It has been said that a person all wrapped up in self makes much too small a package to serve as a partner.

All the dangerous items mentioned above can be discovered courtesy of a relationship X-ray called *Honesty*. A little assistance comes from a reliable search dog called *Truth* that is specifically trained to take a bite out of couple-crime.

Now we must look at the positive side of relationships and outline several articles that are essential for a safe and successful journey.

1. The camera of communication
   Relationship advantage: Clear and frequent communication creates respect and understanding between couples.
2. The headgear of harmony
   Relationship advantage: Harmony involves the creative and intentional combination of personality differences so as to create a symphony of unique characteristics.
3. The fragrance of forgiveness
   Relationship advantage: A willingness to forgive is as valuable within a relationship as a willingness to live. Unforgiveness strangles; forgiveness sets free.
4. The cologne of conflict resolution
   Relationship advantage: It is important to cultivate the ability to go beyond forgiveness and negotiate a constructive mediation for the inevitable differences of opinion that will arise.
5. The satin sheets of self-esteem
   Relationship advantage: You must truly appreciate yourself before you can truly appreciate another person.
6. The traveler's check of faith
   Relationship advantage: Faith in God is the solid foundation upon which to build a reliable relationship that will stand the test of time.

With these and other essential articles in place, the journey is much more likely to be filled with pleasant memories for years to come.

DELIGHTFULLY DIFFERENT

One can find much to read on the intriguing subject of male-female differences. John Gray's best-selling book *Men Are from Mars, Women Are from Venus* is a prime example.[4] One of the often-mentioned physiological differences between the sexes is that women tend to emphasize more "right brain" characteristics such as caring and emotion. Men seem to emphasize more "left brain" tendencies such as logic and problem solving. We will delve further into these gender differences later, but first we must express a disclaimer of sorts. That is, it must be understood that in any such discussion we are dealing with generalities. Many factors such as education, experience, and emotional or spiritual maturity come into play to alter or reverse these generalities for specific persons. Various reasons can be offered for gender contrast, from historical socialization to differences in body shape. The subject of gender differences can stir intense feelings and debate, but our discussion is directly in line with one of the intentions of this book: to provoke the reader to positive action.

CONTRAST #1

Men tend to be goal/task/challenge-oriented;
Women tend to be experience/detail-oriented.

Have you ever noticed how most men somehow find a way to make a game out of everything? The reason is that men are goal-oriented by nature. Some sisters with lazy male friends may disagree. However, even the brother who appears to have no immediate life direction in this decade may exhibit goal-consciousness in areas that seem insignificant to another person, such as sports or automobiles.

One example of goal orientation in men is often displayed on highway trips. A man may attempt to make the trip in record time just to break his previous mark and brag to friends about the accomplishment. How will a woman handle such a situation? A couple could be driving down a freeway, and the woman may lovingly ask her man, "Baby, do you remember what happened here two years ago when we made this trip?" The nondetailed man may not have a clue. Or the woman may view an interstate trip as a wonderful opportunity to be close to her man, admire the beautiful scenery, and to stop at the great outlet malls along the way. She's interested in more than just getting to their destination.

Or consider a shopping trip to the mall. The typical man who goes shopping alone usually knows exactly what he wants and where he intends to get it. He goes directly to the shirt, buys it, and leaves the mall—in record time. A woman may in fact quickly find the skirt or blouse she will end up buying. But no matter how much she likes it, she usually looks around at others before making the purchase.

When it comes to living space, a single man may settle for wall posters for art, planks and cinder blocks for a bookshelf, and second-hand furniture. But when it comes to the stereo system, nothing but totally high tech will do. One way to discern a woman's touch within a home is the distinct attention to the details. Men are concerned about performance and functionality whereas women tend to pay more attention to appearance and ambience.

CONTRAST #2

Men sometimes view sex as a thrilling power play that relieves a load and achieves a goal.

Women tend to view sex as a fulfilling experience of sharing intimacy and giving of self.

Sex is one area that could stand some improvement in the male category. The sharp contrasts between men and women are often the source of trouble in sexual relationships, especially among singles. We will explore this subject further in chapters 3 and 4.

CONTRAST #3

In decision making, men tend to be more analytical and respond with their heads.

In decision making, women are often intuitive and respond with their hearts.

Have you noticed that when children have questions, they often go to their fathers for answers because Daddy knows everything. But when the same children have hurts, they look for mothers because Mama can cure anything. This typifies the differences in how men and women respond to a dilemma. Usually if someone takes a life problem to a man, that person will receive an earful of free advice. Men tend to emphasize individual opinion. When a woman is approached with the problems of life, there is usually an instinctive heart reaction that emotionally pulls her into the situation and causes her to sympathize with the other person. Women tend to be more sensitive to and concerned about the feelings and perceptions of others.

Here is another example of gender differences: Men typically respond to anger and emotion with silence or physical action. John

Gray refers to this as men going into their "caves."[5] Conversely, women tend to react to anger and emotion with many words and much intensity.

CONTRAST #4

A man's sense of self-worth tends to be connected to career/position.
A woman's sense of self-worth tends to be connected to relationships/family.

Get a group of men who are strangers in a room together and the initial conversation is likely to center around what each person does for a living or the various organizations to which they belong. Men tend to place significant emphasis on position and may equate personal position with self-worth. This explains why men tend to become utterly devastated upon losing a job; they may well view it as a loss of significance. At times like this, a man needs sensitivity and encouragement from the women in his life as well as from his male friends. For women, a career can certainly be important, but it usually does not supersede the value placed on the man in her life, her children, or the rest of the extended family.

CONTRAST #5

Men have a great need to be in charge and respected.
Women have a great need for understanding and special treatment.

One of the worst things a woman can do to a man is to disrespect him, especially if he is "dissed" in public and in front of friends. Disrespect is a big issue among and between many minority men. Perhaps there are historical factors in this in that many minority males have grown up in communities where their respect was one of the few things left to call their own. In one of my visits to a maximum-security prison, I encountered a young brother who told me he was incarcerated because he killed a man. Although I usually make it a point not to discuss causes for incarceration, I felt compelled to continue. "Why did you kill him?" I asked. After a brief, reflective pause, he confided, "He disrespected me." I couldn't resist asking what the deceased had specifically done. Even more hesitantly, the inmate replied, "He spit on me." The incident seemed to have occurred inside a pool hall, apparently with a group of peers looking on. What an unnecessarily high price for a man to pay for one moment of disrespect.

On a lighter note, consider the habit of men to not ask for directions. The next time you are heading for an unfamiliar place and your man is driving and you notice that you're seeing the same houses and yards for the third or fourth time, how will you as a woman react? You could instruct, criticize, or loudmouth your man. But to restore his self-confidence, why not simply sit back, relax, enjoy the beautiful scenery, and exude an unmistakable air of confidence that your man will get you there . . . eventually. This simple gesture greatly appeals to the pride of the man who reads this as your respect of his ability to reach his goal.

While a woman usually has no problem accepting help with directions, she does have her own set of concerns. An example is her strong need to be understood and to be treated like a treasure. This treatment need not be exorbitant and elaborate. It could assume the form of a phone call in the middle of the day just to say, "I was just sitting here at work thinkin' 'bout ya and wanted you to know that you were on my mind." Or it could be as simple as a handwritten note, left on her car windshield or secretly tucked into her coat pocket, expressing your sincere appreciation for the precious time the two of you share together. A man can hardly go wrong with any gesture that communicates the message that "you are not generic, but of designer quality; you deserve to be handled with care and treated with dignity because there is only one like you." Try it. She'll like it.

FOR MEN ONLY: WHAT A WOMAN WON'T TELL YOU
(BUT WISHES YOU ALREADY KNEW)

In his book *Race Matters*, Cornel West cites three ways in which Black women have been negatively stereotyped: "There is Jezebel (the seductive temptress), Sapphira (the evil manipulator), or Aunt Jemima (the sexless, long-suffering nurturer)."[6]

The problem with all stereotypes is that they fall short of capturing the true, holistic essence and variety of that which they attempt to represent. Historically Blacks have been characterized not in the framework of humanity, but in the framework of generality and caricature.

If one person consistently thinks of another in terms of a stereotype or a caricature, it is much easier to dismiss that individual's personhood and thus devalue him or her to a nonentity.

Unfortunately, the same pattern of persecution historically perpetrated on African-Americans is comparable to the contemporary pattern exhibited by some African-American men with regard to Black women. But the marvelously incredible reality is that Black women have endured and persevered through so many life tribulations with a significant measure of sanity, tolerance, and understanding still left. It is amazing what a Black woman can take yet remain standing and singing and desiring to make things work in spite of the obvious odds against her. But, brothers, these sisters are getting tired. You can see it in the hand on the hip, the curl of the mouth, the swaying of the neck, and the cutting of the eyes. "Relationship recess" is over, and it's time to get serious about not taking women for granted and providing them with what they need and deserve in a man. We as men must develop and demonstrate the attitude that it is a privilege just to be in their presence. This attitude is what Gary Smalley refers to as creating an atmosphere of "honor" for your mate or date.[7]

Popular opinion holds that the most important items on a Black woman's short list of desirable qualities in a man are the notorious twin attributes of a prestigious position and a substantial income. However, the research for this book included a survey of more than 250 single, college-aged Black women, and among other questions they were asked about the personal qualities they appreciated and considered most important in a dating partner. The results were surprising—and reflect the first thing that a woman may not tell you but wishes you already knew. Each group surveyed consistently reflected a feminine preference for the two simple human qualities of honesty and trustworthiness. These two important characteristics are conspicuously absent from most of the high-profile role models observed through television, movies, music, and sports.

These two characteristics of trust and honesty are really two sides of the same quality. Women seek these traits in men for two reasons: First, trust and honesty are essential. It is impossible to build a safe and reliable relationship without these qualities. Like a house, many relationships that appeared to be inviting and impressive on the outside have been occupied for a season, only to eventually collapse due to the absence of the rafters of honesty and the support beams of trust.

Second, these traits are too often absent, with grave consequences, in the relationships with the men in their lives, whether these men are fathers or boyfriends or spouses. Many women are unconsciously searching for someone to fill the gigantic vacuum left behind by a man who failed to fulfill his role as father. Many unsuspecting suitors find themselves dealing with the casualties of relationships past. The deep-seated pain caused by absentee or inadequate fatherhood is aptly underscored by entertainer Halle Berry, who expressed her reflections on her divorce in an *Essence* magazine interview:

> Berry says her father failed to provide her with the kind of healthy nurturing relationship that would have served as a template for her adult relationships with men. Had he been there for her, she would have had a much better chance of marching out of her childhood empowered by the love of a responsible man who adored her. Instead, her dad's betrayal may have left an innocent child feeling unworthy and vulnerable in a way that will take years to overcome. She admits that she took a little girl's yearning for a daddy into her marriage, expecting her husband to fill the void. "I realize now that what I really wanted was a good father. I see good fathering as unconditional love from a man. . . . David [her former husband] needed a good father himself. His dad hadn't been around either. I was asking a man to be something that he had no frame of reference for. We both wanted the same things and didn't know how to get them from each other."[8]

Just as a surgeon is not allowed to operate on the heart of a patient without a significant amount of training and prior observation, we as men should take our cue from this example and be determined not to inflict permanent emotional damage on the life of any woman due to our careless and haphazard handling of her heart. A man's words and the way he says them carry considerable weight. Women are sensitive to speech and the tone of words. Men sometimes take unfair advantage of this condition and may tell a woman what he knows she wants to hear, without regard for the truth. This can lead to her agreeing to things that she would not ordinarily do under different conditions. Of course, the opposite extreme of this stance can be equally as harmful when "brutal honesty" is used. Even though something may be true about a person, that does not give us permission to be insensitive and cruel with our honesty. The key is to be truthful without being brutal.

Another small but potentially misleading gesture is the manner in which we nonsexually touch a woman. A gentle massage of her neck, a tender caress of her hand, or the graceful embrace of her waist may send a strong message of love and commitment when our intention was not nearly that serious. As you have probably observed, women in general tend to become emotionally attached faster than men. One of the reasons for this seems to be the strong feminine desire for security and stability.

Most women have a high need to feel safe, protected, and assured. Although my wife and I live in what I consider a very safe neighborhood, at bedtime she periodically asks me, "Are all the doors locked?" Even though I am not as concerned as she, I usually get up anyway and check the lock for her sake because it means a lot to her.

FOR WOMEN ONLY: WHAT A MAN WON'T ADMIT
(BUT HOPES YOU'LL FIGURE OUT)

Black men have historically shouldered their share of myths and stereotypes. These stereotypes range from strong, young stud/buck and hilarious buffoon to pretty boy pimp/player and dangerous/unpredictable predator. Without a doubt the primary images of Black men have been predominantly negative and distasteful. The challenge at hand is to move beyond these limited images, which are often reinforced by the entertainment world and disproportionately highlighted by the media. The powerful imitative atmosphere among young Black males can turn negative stereotypes into self-fulfilling prophecies. Due to a lack of healthy, constantly accessible role models within many elements of the Black community, Black boys tend to turn to the closest male with the highest profile. Whereas the Black male with the highest profile used to be the local pastor, more recently it proves to be a professional athlete or—much worse—the community cocaine king-pin.

It is difficult to know how to successfully fulfill a role for which there have been largely poor examples if any at all. This condition in itself is an overwhelmingly compelling reason to strive for more posi-tive Black male examples in the media and the community. Without these positive role models the unhealthy patterns will continue. The average male will not risk being vulnerable enough to admit that he does not truly know what it means to be a positive, functional partner in a relationship—especially in a marriage. This is one reason that men-torship is an important and potentially transforming practice. If more Black young men were paired with seasoned and commendable Black family men who have developed a productive relationship with their mates, what a difference there would be in a matter of months.

Another issue that a man will probably not admit but hopes you will somehow figure out is that Black men are not just out looking for sex. After you recover from your state of shock or your fit of hysterical laughter, consider that the statement is actually the title of a powerful book by Alvis O. Davis: *Black Men Not Looking for Sex.*[9]

Have you ever heard of a man who had boasted of "playing around" a lot and then one day decided to settle down with just one woman? Perhaps he explained this sudden change in behavior by saying, "Man, I finally found what I was looking for!" If this statement is true, then casual sex was evidently something he wanted at one time—but what was he ultimately looking for? This difference in nuance is very subtle but extremely important for women to understand in negotiating healthy and mutually beneficial relationships with men. Many female hearts have been broadsided because they misunderstood and misin-terpreted this small-but-important difference. Davis explains it well:

> It is often not until their heart is broken that [women] learn that giving sex to a black man may get them some things, but long-term commitment is usually not one of them. Many women are duped into establishing a "sexship" instead of a well-balanced, committed relationship. A sexship is what a man establishes when he communicates with a woman primarily to

have sex with her. Sometimes black men do whatever it takes to keep a sexship sailing—and no more. One way you know you're in a sexship is that you're having sex with him and he's not committed to you. Because the focus is often on temporary physical gratification, very few sexships progress into long-term, committed, quality relationships. Sexships commonly serve as a vehicle for black men to validate their manhood and to live up to the confines of the image. Beware! Sexships come and go. Most invariably end up sinking, and quite often taking someone's heart down with them.[10]

A man may *want* sex as a temporary thrill, but if he is looking for a permanent relationship, sex is not the primary drawing factor.

Please don't miss this rare and priceless perspective. As Davis aptly observes, "Black women are often rudely awakened to discover that many Black men will do much more for them in pursuit of sex than they will after sex."[11] This may be hard to understand and believe, but if a man truly appreciates a woman, he may try to make a sexual move on her just to "see what she is made of." If he truly likes her for more than her body, he will actually be disappointed if she gives in to him; he will be more motivated to stay in the relationship if she holds out. He will not tell her this in words, but he hopes she will figure it out. Davis continues,

> If you do give in, and sex becomes the center of attention and the main attraction, other facets of what might have been a good relationship will start to suffer primarily because you gave him what he wanted and not what he was looking for.[12]

This same line of reasoning extends to the clothing. Some women make the mistake of thinking, "If I dress provocatively with my cleavage visible, my thighs showing, and my midriff bare, I will attract a lot of attention." Of course this attracts attention. The question is, what *kind* of attention will it attract? Believe me, most men will not approach a provocatively dressed woman with anything except a game mentality and an exploitative motive. It is the same mind-set with which a gambler approaches a slot machine or a blackjack table: "You may end up using me but I'm sure going to try to use you first." If you respect yourself and demonstrate that respect in everything you do, most men will return that respect. Your view of yourself will significantly affect their treatment of you.

CONCLUSION

It is time for Black men and women to commit to being *for* each other—not against each other. We must become lifetime allies rather than enemies. But this will come only through making an effort to understand each other.

If we are to succeed in the future, we will succeed *together*.

LET'S TALK!

1. How does 1 Corinthians 12:7–12 relate to the subject of male-female differences?
2. Do you feel that there is a significant problem with communication in most male-female relationships? Why or why not?
3. In what ways has your view of the other gender been shaped by the influence of your parents?
4. In what ways have your attitude and behavior toward the other gender been shaped by the media?
5. If you walked through a "relationship X-ray" security-check area, what specific kinds of "violations" might be discovered?
6. What is the strongest asset or characteristic that you can contribute to a male-female relationship?
7. Briefly review the male-female contrasts offered in this chapter. Which ones have you exhibited yourself or observed in others?
8. Is there one or more of the suggested contrasts with which you disagree? Explain.
9. Discuss the potential challenges and benefits of combining goal orientation and experience orientation in a relationship.
10. Discuss the possible challenges and benefits of confronting both logical and intuitive tendencies in a relationship.
11. Discuss imaginative ways by which a woman can show respect to a man and by which a man can show a woman she is special.

Chapter 3

NO CONDOM FOR THE MIND

The Myths of So-called Safe Sex

When the HIV/AIDS virus began its devastation in America in the 1980s, a new phrase was devised in an attempt to stem the rapidly increasing onslaught of new cases. The term was initially called "safe sex," and more recently has been altered to "safer sex." I have always been a bit skeptical of the implications of the terms, especially the latter one. Upon hearing it, I reasoned, "If I were to jump from an airplane while on a skydiving expedition, would I want to take a chance on using a parachute marked 'safer parachute'? Since I would be risking my life in this experience, I think I would want one of the *safest* parachutes.

Premarital sex these days is becoming increasingly comparable to skydiving. There is the exciting anticipation of the ascent and the danger and thrill of the jump—but there is also a much higher occurrence of fatal crash landings with premarital sex than with parachuting.

"Recreational sex" can be compared to cotton candy at a summer carnival. The experience is exciting and the taste is sweet, but the pleasure is short-lived and provides no adequate nourishment. Bonnie Pfister captures the essence of the matter as she writes, "Sex is perfectly natural, but not naturally perfect."[1] A good thing can become a bad thing if not handled correctly. Many problems can occur when couples proceed too quickly from "lip service" to "hip service." In such cases, safe sex is not always the cure-all. In his article "Sexuality on Campus," Toby Simon displays keen insight into the situation:

It's easy to understand how anyone gets carried away in the throes of passion. The intensity of the moment can make it difficult for people to stop doing what they are doing to talk about protection and find a condom.... Sex feels good, and the part of the body that feels the best has no brain. As a result, unprotected intercourse takes place, and a variety of outcomes follow. It is often after one such passionate unprotected love making session that students decide to be more cautious next time.[2]

Bishop Larry Trotter of the Full Gospel Baptist Church also describes this seemingly ever-present urge to merge. He says it is

... when your hormones are calling for a response that will satisfy your flesh.... when you feel like you're out of control and you need sex to bring you back into control.... when your spirit man has been overridden by your natural man.... when you can't seem to think of anything else but being sexually satisfied.... when you feel a need to run through your old phone book to find somebody to talk to.... when you are so lonely that you desire closeness with another person to the point that you are driven by passion. [It] is that state that you get in and no matter what you do, you still have "hot flashes" or moments of erotic thoughts.... that state of mind that hinders you at that time from thinking about anything else other than your desires.... when your flesh is totally out of control.[3]

Now that the sexual urge has been quite adequately described, let us delve into the possible motives behind initial sexual experiences. In my research for this book, a number of Black college students were asked, "On your first occasion of sexual intercourse, what was your main reason?" The highest percentage (34%) identified "curiosity" as the primary reason, followed by "love/affection for my partner" (11%). A similar national survey indicates that the top reason among women for having initial consensual intercourse is affection for partner (48%), but for men the top reason is curiosity/readiness for sex (a whopping 51%).[4] This sounds as if a great many people are the unwary subjects of sexual experiments by unlicensed practitioners. My survey shows that even after the initial encounters, the main reasons given for continuing with premarital sex are love for the partner (47%) and a strong desire for sex (21%). Would you like to examine your attitude and motives relating to sexual intercourse? Check the single category that most closely reflects your opinion as to when sex is acceptable to you:

_____ 1. When in love

_____ 2. When desire is strong

_____ 3. When the feeling is right

_____ 4. Within a strong relationship

_____ 5. Within a strong marriage

_____ 6. When both partners are mature enough

_____ 7. Not sure

_____ 8. Other _____

Whatever we do in life, we should have a good reason for doing it. This is especially true with an experience as volatile as sexual intercourse. Even with the use of a condom, several potential problems still exist such as improper usage, infrequent usage, rare manufacturing defects, or breaks and spills. In addition, there is the seldom-mentioned consideration that there is no condom for emotional pain, no protection for the mind. The sexual act was designed as the most intimate physical, psychological, and spiritual experience possible between a man and a woman. Sometimes one person invests a great deal in the relationship, becoming giving and vulnerable. When the other partner invests less and abandons the relationship or betrays the trust, there is no condom manufactured that will offer protection from that kind of pain. Consider that for unmarried couples living together, the average length of their relationship is about one year.[5] Even if they eventually marry, their marriages tend to be less stable than for those who do not live together before marriage.[6]

SEXUALITY AMONG COLLEGE STUDENTS

College students rank higher than average for risk of HIV infection. Robert R. Redfield Jr. is an AIDS research professional who estimates that the next wave of increased HIV infection levels will be among African-American college students.[7] This is understandable considering the high rates of sexual activity on many college campuses. In a study of risk behavior among students, it was concluded that the "sensation seeking predisposition" of college students combined with a "sexual motive for a pleasurable relationship" has a direct effect upon all areas of their sexual behavior, including number of partners and incidents of unprotected sex.[8]

According to *Change* magazine, "On college campuses, alcohol is often a factor in sexual misadventures ranging from unanticipated sexual activity to unprotected activity and acquaintance rape."[9] With literally thousands of college students simultaneously attempting to become comfortable with their sexuality along with confronting many other challenges, alcohol is often a factor in just "letting sex happen." One campus survey reported that 47% of students had participated in sex when they had not planned to, but did so as a result of alcohol. Alcohol impairs one's ability even to remember to discuss the use of birth control.[10]

On the college campuses there can be tremendous pressure to lose one's virginity, especially among freshmen. Most are very eager to become accepted by their new college peer group. Men in particular are subject to ridicule over their virginity. As a result, they may find themselves engaging in sexual activity that they did not really want but did not know how to tactfully decline. College students today have too often grown up in a culture that promotes male sexual aggression and positively reinforces the notion that "real men" are sexually active, always ready, and programmed never to say no to sex.[11]

Sex is still the number-one issue that college students desire to discuss. Alan Guskin, president of Antioch College, states, "Sexuality is perhaps the most defining issue for today's students."[12] Any force possessing power—such as wind, water, or fire—has the potential to be either harmful or helpful. The factor that determines the outcome is the presence or absence of discipline. When sexuality submits to discipline, its bestiality begins to wane and its beauty begins to rise. Sexual discipline is a mature call for the exercising of willpower as well as what Jan Farrington describes as "won't power."[13] This discipline includes the right and the strength to say no even if one has said yes in the past.

SEVEN SYMPTOMS OF SEXUAL MISUSE

Specific reasons that singles desire or consent to sexual intercourse are as varied as human personality itself. However, many of the reasons fall within the scope of the categories examined below. Some may seem totally reasonable, while others may seem at first glance ridiculous. Whatever the case, let us explore the intricacies of each reason given.

1. SEX AS RECREATIONAL RELEASE

Without a doubt, the physical urge for sex is very strong. Our God-given hormones dutifully accomplish their assigned task of fueling our innate urge to merge sexually. Like an athlete naturally driven to play sports, some singles view sex as an entertaining game to be played; a natural and spontaneous reaction to a basic human drive. The problem with this point of view is that many make the mistake of separating the sexual urge from all other human needs. For example, every human has a need to eat food. But directly related to this is the need for discipline:

—Eating the correct kinds of food (to avoid unhealthy intake)
—Eating the correct amounts of food (to avoid being underfed or overfed)
—Eating an appropriate variety of foods (to ensure a balanced diet)
—Eating at the appropriately spaced times (to assist in proper digestion)

Just as it would be unwise to eat without restraint or discipline, similarly it would be a mistake to view sex as an isolated need to be fulfilled without regard to surrounding circumstances. Sex can be of maximum benefit or of maximum harm, depending on several conditions. Those who view sex as a sport understand that, like other competitive games such as football or basketball, most instances of "recreational sex" have a winner and a loser. With this mind-set comes an exotic collection of relationship gaming behaviors that do very little to foster healthy communication, build trust, and promote true intimacy.

Some singles have never been exposed to beneficial examples of male-female relationships and have only observed relationships riddled with the bullet holes of gaming behavior. The damaging result is an emotionally wounded generation with an unhealthy relationship style that is destined to be passed to future generations unless we break the cycle and increase the peace among Black men and women. We are not each other's enemies; we must become each other's friends.

2. SEX AS A SAMPLE

A popular ice-cream establishment boasts thirty-one flavors to offer customers. Upon entering the store one is sometimes overwhelmed by the wide variety; it's difficult to choose just one flavor. The management's awareness of this dilemma of indecision prompted them to simplify the selection process by providing small spoons for customer taste-tests and samples. There does not seem to be a particular limit on the number of sample spoons allowed, and one might be tempted to sample as many flavors as possible.

Some singles tend to view sex this way. On college campuses and elsewhere there is any variety of people who reflect the following characteristics:

—They are often single and searching.
—They are often experiencing new freedom and seeking to discover new things.
—They are often highly susceptible to peer pressure.
—They are often at their sexual prime and willing to take chances.
—There are often surrounded by a highly social, party atmosphere.
—They often have a wide range of potential partners from which to choose.

The difficulties with curiosity-driven "sample sex" are many. First, there are the obvious health risks associated with casual sex. Second, repeated behavior tends to forge a pattern that can be very difficult to break once one finally decides to "settle down." Third, sample sex reduces the sacredness of the sexual encounter to a generic, low-budget level. Other problems with this attitude will be addressed later in this chapter.

3. SEX AS A RITE OF PASSAGE

Virgin is not a dirty word. Rather, it is a beautiful, sensuous, attractive, exciting, mysterious, alluring, and provocative word. However, some people seem to think that losing one's virginity is synonymous with "becoming a man" or "becoming a woman." Such sentiments reflect a lack of understanding as to what it truly takes to make a woman a woman and a man a man. If a person is not mature before lying down, the sexual act will not itself produce maturity. In other words, sex alone is not a truly authentic rite of passage.

To become really mature, try starting a business, "adopting" a senior citizen, becoming a Big Brother or Big Sister, volunteering at a prison, or starting a feeding-clothing program for the homeless. It is responsibility, not sexuality, that helps to develop a balanced maturity. Don't buy the lie and become another casualty in the long line of men and women who have fallen for the empty "rite of passage" promise usually made by a selfish partner. You may well awaken the morning after, alone in bed, clutching a pillow wet with the tears of a broken dream and a disappointing sexual experience that did not quite go as portrayed in the movies.

4. SEX AS A THANK YOU

There are many ways to say thank you. Unfortunately, sex has become a common way to express appreciation for flowers, a dinner, a dance, or a movie. Such a shallow attitude toward such a sacred act classifies "thank-you sex" as nothing more than "glorified prostitution." Instead of being offered in exchange for money, sex is exchanged for time, attention, food, or entertainment.

If the gift of sex is shared in exchange for such small commitments, what incentive is there to make greater commitments? Tangled feelings and irregular relationship development are the unfortunate result of sex out of context. The mere fact that two people consent to share their precious time with each other should be thanks enough. Don't give up your body for a burger! Relationships may come and go, but there is only one you. It is unwise to exchange that which is passing for that which is priceless.

5. SEX AS RELATIONSHIP INSURANCE

Some people pay a high price in an effort to keep a relationship from dissolving. The line of reasoning goes something like this: "If I give him/her a little 'nookie' here and there, his/her mind is less likely to wander and he/she will want to stay with me." The problem with this "logic" is that everyone else has basically the same "nookie" as you have. You run the risk of becoming "old nookie" and being abandoned in a search for some "new nookie."

Another side to this concept of sex as relationship insurance is that intercourse is designed to bind a man and a woman together in a holy and permanent relationship. The problem is that some of this binding begins to take place whether or not the relationship is holy or permanent. The frequent result is an extremely intense, intangible "soul tie" between two who have united themselves sexually. Since soul ties are strong and not easily broken, the wisest option is to wait for the commitment of marriage.

6. SEX AS REBELLION, REVENGE, OR RANSOM

Out-of-context-sex is sometimes displayed in the form of a relationship power play in protest or retaliation for being angered or hurt by another person. The three forms of this type of behavior are "rebellion sex," "revenge sex," and "ransom sex."

Rebellion sex is typically seen among young adults who are making an effort to sever the parental apron strings. Indiscriminate sex is often used to defiantly affirm adulthood and independence from parental authority. There are two reasons for this. First, sex is usually the most dreaded subject for many parents, and the son or daughter knows that to become promiscuous would be like hitting them with a one-megaton bomb. Second, sex is often the nearest substitute for the personal attention, affirmation, and genuine intimacy they subconsciously crave.

Revenge sex can be explained through the following example. Two people, whom we will call Bo and Sasha, had been in an exclusive relationship for two years. Sasha was looking forward to the royal treatment by Bo on her birthday just as he had done the year before. Last year he had surprised her with a bouquet of flowers and a ride in a chauffeur-driven stretch limousine to an exquisite Italian restaurant. That was followed by a midnight cruise on a riverboat, where they took turns gently tossing rose petals into the water, each with a tender wish for their future together. With each day, her excitement and anticipation increased as to how Bo would top last year's birthday tribute. But she said nothing to him because of her great love for surprises.

When the big day finally arrived, she put on the new dress that she had purchased on her summer trip to New York. That black dress hugged her curves like a Porsche on a winding mountain road. She couldn't resist pausing briefly as she passed by her full-length mirror. As she gazed approvingly, she softly whispered, "Go girl!" Bo and Sasha had a "standing date" every Saturday at the same time, and as the seven o'clock hour rolled around, Sasha had "conveniently" scheduled for three of her girlfriends to stop by and pick up a videotape shortly before Bo was to arrive.

Well, Bo showed up right on time—dressed to the nines in his cutoff sweat pants, sweaty tank top, Air Jordans, and a gym bag over his shoulder. Tiffany was the first to spot him walking up to the door and asked Sasha if *he* knew where *they* were going. Sasha didn't even understand the question until she opened the door. Sasha and Bo simply stared at each other for fifteen awkward seconds—which was just long enough for it to click in Bo's head as to what day it was. Try as he might to explain that he had forgotten all about the birthday and had just come from the gym after several games with the fellas and that if she would just wait there a couple of hours he would be right back for her and they would go out on the town and have the best . . . SLAM!

The echo of the door reverberated in Bo's ears as he slowly walked back to his Jeep. Sasha, with steely eyes, assured her friends that she would be all right. The door had barely shut behind them as Sasha reached for her address book. She called a number that she had written there three years ago. "Calvin" answered with his customary, mellow "Talk to me." Recognizing Sasha's voice, he immediately said, "I was just thinking about you today. Happy birthday!" Within two minutes Calvin had been invited over to help Sasha "celebrate." Calvin promised to be there just as soon as he finished showering from his sweaty basketball game with Bo and the fellas. That night Calvin was a somewhat willing "victim" of "revenge sex" as Sasha sought to hurt Bo as badly as she had been hurt by him.

The drawback of revenge sex is that it does not solve the original problem and the problems it causes are often greater than the pain originally inflicted. The result is a tangled web of pain and problems.

Ransom sex refers to withholding sexual favors as a way of inflicting misery on a partner who is accustomed to sex upon desire or request. What happens is that the partner who has been offended decides to "kidnap" his or her own body and hold it hostage until an acceptable "ransom" is paid. The person withholding sex may continue to do so until he or she receives an apology or a "peace offering" or simply gets over the anger. This, too, is a misuse of sex and falls far short of the original intention.

7. SEX AS A SUBSTITUTE FOR INTIMACY

Perhaps the most frequent and flagrant misuse of sex is as a substitute for intimacy. Another name for it could be "sex as a quick fix" because of the tendency to use sex as a universal tool to smooth over almost any problem. Intimacy is that unquenchable thirst for oneness with someone else. It is the deep desire to reach, risk, know, and be known. It is to understand and to be understood by someone who can always be counted upon to "have your back." Rick Stedman accurately identifies this quest for intimacy in his delightfully insightful book, *Pure Joy! The Positive Side of Single Sexuality.*

> An emotion similar to intimacy is felt when clothing is removed, and each person reveals what is kept from public view. A feeling of closeness is sometimes experienced when two people lie down side by side, touching and being touched. A sense of being cherished is approximated by the intensity with which the two cling to one another, holding each other tightly. But the myth is ultimately false. Sex does not necessarily provide intimacy. Instead it can prevent true intimacy from ever occurring, genuine vulnerability from happening, authentic closeness from being achieved. In the wrong context, sex can be the enemy of intimacy.[14]

Later in the book Stedman compares and contrasts intimacy and sexual desire:

> Humans are physically drawn to others not just to satisfy physical desire and not merely to keep the species alive. In the drama of human history, sexual desire and procreation are

really just minor-player publicity-seeking prima donnas who, much to their disappointment, are only given bit parts. The major character, the real star on the stage of human history, corresponds to the major theme, the desire for interpersonal intimacy. The most important actor is the hunger for interpersonal closeness that most strongly attracts us to one another. It is the thirst for a communion of souls that motivates us to love in spite of the fear of failure.[15]

Perhaps the most tragic aspect of all seven symptoms of sex out of context is that no one need settle for so little when life can offer so much more. Most people settle for substitutes for intimacy, not because they cannot afford the real thing, but because they are unaware of how to secure the real thing. The ingredients of intimacy are found far beyond superficial appearance or sexual technique.

LET'S TALK!

1. Read 1 Thessalonians 4:3–7. What does it mean to "take advantage" of someone else?
2. Discuss the implications of this statement: "Sex is perfectly natural, but not naturally perfect."
3. What are the advantages and disadvantages of so-called safe-sex claims?
4. Which category at the beginning of the chapter most closely reflects your opinion as to when sex is acceptable to you? Elaborate.
5. Do you think that "recreational sex" is more prevalent on the college campus than elsewhere? Why or why not?
6. Which of the seven symptoms of sexual misuse do you think is the most common? How can it be addressed?
7. What is your image of and your feelings about a female virgin who is over the age of twenty-one?
8. What is your image of and your feelings about a male virgin who is over the age of twenty-one?
9. Were your answers the same for questions 6 and 7? Explain.

10. Do you feel obligated to respond physically on an expensive date? Do you feel you deserve to receive some physical touch when you were the one doing the spending?
11. What are the primary issues and mistakes involved in the scenario with Bo, Sasha, and Calvin?

Chapter 4

SANCTIFIED SEX
The Delights of Deferred Gratification

In normal conversation the words *sanctified* and *sex* are seldom mentioned in the same sentence, much less as joint noun and adjective. In the Black community these words are especially separated because the word *sanctified* has been historically associated with a particular type of church or worship style. However, *sanctified* actually means "clean, purified, consecrated, holy, dedicated."[1]

Given the continuing decline of decency in American society, it is difficult for us to imagine anything connected with sex as clean or consecrated. Many people feel that God either begrudgingly tolerates or completely condemns expressions of sexuality. But God invented sexuality. Sex was God's idea originally. Sadly, however, all great ideas are subject to abuse. The Chinese who invented explosives for fireworks never intended them to be used with firearms to take human lives. Henry Ford never intended his automobiles to be used by intoxicated drivers to cause many deaths.[2] Likewise, when God invented sexuality, God created it to be good. And it is still good when in the right context.

Let us pursue a better understanding of sexuality through first viewing it from a wider perspective. One's total sexuality is everything that makes a woman a woman and everything that makes a man a man. Sexuality is therefore part of one's total personhood. So often, sexuality has been equated with intercourse alone. Because of this, many fail to realize the wide variety of ways to intimately relate that do not involve physical contact. Sexuality and interpersonal intimacy may be communicated on an endless variety of levels, including social, recreational, aesthetic, and intellectual.

Three primary ways of communicating intimacy and sexuality are physically, emotionally, and spiritually. When our sexual relationship is only one-dimensional, it is much more likely to break when pressure is applied. In the book *Sexual Character*, Marva Dawn exposes what happens when sexual union is overemphasized as opposed to the development of the whole relationship:

> Because deep inside we know that our lives are less intimate than they need to be, we try to create that intimacy, but we don't know how to do it in any other ways than through technique. For example, sexual union, which is most satisfying as the culminating expression of growing intimacy in many human dimensions, has been ripped out of that context and placed as the initiating act for relationships. Since it then has no corresponding intimacies, improvements must deal with the very act itself, and consequently we have to write manuals on techniques to make "sex" more exciting. This is the wrong remedy for our emotional aches. The true source of pain has not been diagnosed.[3]

Dawn affirms that intercourse was designed as a sign of marital union, then shows how we must look beyond the sign itself and concentrate on the essence to which the sign points. Without the essence, the sign is an empty and useless symbol. Such a useless sign can be illustrated through the scenario of a car full of travelers in search of a certain hotel who pull over to park after seeing a sign announcing that the hotel is five miles away.

Genital union was not designed to mark the initiation of a serious relationship, but rather to accent the consummation or crowning activity of a permanently committed, divinely orchestrated relationship. Of course, the rite of marriage alone does not guarantee intimacy any more than intercourse guarantees intimacy. The most important elements in a successful marriage or relationship are commitment, communication, honesty, trust, respect, mutual goals and interests, a sense of humor, forgiveness, and obedience to God's will. These qualities are not for the immature. They require a tremendous amount of work to maintain, can be emotionally draining to sustain, and are most successfully accomplished in an environment of security, permanence, honor, commitment, and godliness. Otherwise, we feel vulnerable and tend to hold back from our partner.

Sanctified sex is sexual intercourse accompanied by the awesome qualities listed above. When these qualities form the framework for the bonding of the bodies, the sexual act holds a satisfaction that cannot exist otherwise. Consider the following comparison between the ills typical of premarital sex and the thrills of sanctified sex:

Typical sex often ...
    Steals the relationship show
    Kills genuine friendship
    Grills true intimacy
    Spills patience
    Deals the unexpected
    Wills pain when the relationship dies
Sanctified sex often ...
    Builds trust
    Heals doubts and hurts
    Fills voids
    Seals discipline
    Shields from relationship predators
    Yields to God

Sanctified sex is a way of understanding and relating to our partner that involves tenderness, care, concern, vulnerability, personal and joint development, intimacy, and spiritual growth. For singles, sanctified sex does not require genital contact with a partner; rather, it exercises the virtues of patience and self-discipline all the way to the marriage altar.

The term *sanctified sex* emerged from my frustration with the terms typically used to express the biblical perspective regarding sexuality. This perspective is usually communicated with words and phrases such as "abstinence," "celibacy," and "just say no." These terms all seem to have a predominantly negative and unattractive connotation. Janie Gustafson echoes the same kind of frustration with regard to how all too many churches address sexuality:

> Although traditional Christian moralists have upheld celibacy as a virtue, they have certainly not presented it as very appealing. I often find their definitions of celibacy negative and empty. . . . It is a sober, somber, bloodless virtue which represses or denies my basic sexuality. . . . My celibacy has got to be passionate, and my passion, my desire for union with another, must have its celibate dimensions. Passion, as I experience it, is not something I consider. . . evil. It is a push, a drive from within, an energy which moves me into relationship with others. It is an intense thirst for intimacy, a yearning for real living, which at the same time affirms and accepts me as separate and individual.[4]

Consistent with this observation, Marva Dawn suggests that if the church in general were more intentional about nurturing the community through offering more affection and care for individuals, "many would be less likely to turn falsely to genital sexual expression for the social support they need."[5]

In light of all this, I looked for a term that could express positive appeal yet maintain the moral ideal. "Sanctified sex" suggests sex that is so precious, powerful, and costly that it is intentionally set apart for special usage.

BENEFITS OF SANCTIFIED SEX

Here are a few practical reasons to invest in sanctified sex:

1. SANCTIFIED SEX PUTS THE SPOTLIGHT ON THE QUALITIES MOST IMPORTANT FOR A HEALTHY RELATIONSHIP.

Let's compare a relationship to a church building. Although the most important part of a structure is its foundation, it is the steeple or spire that gets the most attention. When we are driving toward a city or a small town, the most visible object—the thing we see first—is very likely to be a tower or steeple. Yet, despite the high profile, the truth is that not much of the building's business occurs in the steeple. If the steeple were removed, the building might look less beautiful, but the business for which the building exists could continue unabated. But just try removing the foundation and see what kinds of problems you would encounter. How ironic it is that the most important aspect of a typical building is seldom visible except at the time of initial construction.

A male-female relationship that is built on the steeple of sex is destined to fall. However, when a strong foundation, sturdy walls, and a good roof are all in place, a steeple or tower simply makes a wonderful finishing touch and adds a great deal of beauty. The basics must always precede the beauty. Sanctified sex puts sex in its proper perspective, not as the foundation of the relationship, but as a very beautiful and unique feature.

2. SANCTIFIED SEX HELPS TO DISTINGUISH BETWEEN POTENTIAL PARTNERS WHO ARE SERIOUS AND THOSE WHO ARE MERELY CURIOUS.

When a partner is "rewarded" with sex too soon, the relationship can be short-circuited. If the partner is motivated mainly by sexual curiosity, there would no longer be a compelling reason to remain in the relationship once the curiosity has been satisfied. But if two people genuinely care for each other, the absence of intercourse will not interfere with continued togetherness. In that sense, abstinence helps to promote full-fledged, genuine intimacy.

3. SANCTIFIED SEX BUILDS TRUST AND ENCOURAGES THE HABITUAL PATTERN OF "POSITIVE SEXUAL INERTIA" IN A RELATIONSHIP.

Human beings are creatures of habit. When we perform certain actions a few times in succession, there is a tendency for that pattern to persist. We know that habits can be either positive or negative, healthy or unhealthy, so we need to *en*courage the positive patterns and *dis*courage the negative trends. Many singles naïvely think that they can have a lifestyle of serial sexual partners and then, when they decide to settle down and get married, there will no longer be a tendency or desire to "experiment" sexually. The truth is that old habits die slowly and everything done or not done during the single life has a direct or indirect effect on married life. Isn't it reasonable to think that if a person is unable to control the sex drive while single, significant problems might arise in a marriage if, for example, the partner developed a medical condition that precluded intercourse for a while? What if the spouse had to go on an extended business trip or spend a month out of town to care for a sick relative? To pursue positive patterns while single is to establish positive patterns for marriage.

4. SANCTIFIED SEX HELPS TO PREVENT FLASHBACKS AND SEXUAL COMPARISONS IN THE BEDROOM.

Another natural tendency among human beings is to make comparisons. We compare food, cars, teachers, cities, and personal experiences. Have you ever thought or even said, "My last friend and I didn't really hit it off that well in terms of the relationship, but he/she sure can kiss!" Just as we cannot help but compare kisses, we surely cannot help but compare something as deeply personal as a sexual experience. The only way to prevent sexual comparisons or "ghosts in the bedroom" is to have only one sexual partner in a relationship sanctified by marriage. This way your spouse can qualify as "the world's greatest lover" simply because he or she has set the standard and there is no one else with whom to compare.

5. SANCTIFIED SEX ALLOWS US TO GIVE OUR LIFELONG SOUL MATE THE MOST UNIQUE AND PERSONAL PRESENT OF ALL.

The sexual act is much more than a mutual physical exercise; it is actually a "covenantal sign"[6] that marks the sanctity and sacredness of a marriage. Sex within marriage is a regular reminder of this covenant of oneness. Wedding gifts may come and go, but we can give away our virginity only once and to only one person. As Ray Mossholder puts it, sex is God's wedding gift to the couple.[7] Virgins always have the option of becoming sexually active, but once virginity has been surrendered, it cannot be retrieved. The only option at that point would be a kind of "secondary virginity," as pro-basketball star A. C. Green prefers to call it. In *Jet* magazine Green confirmed that he was a virgin and "proud of it." He explained how as a single man and a public figure he was able to remain a virgin in the midst of many beautiful women:

Easy. I have respect for myself and for the women I have dated. I compare it to a steak and a hamburger. I expect the best for me, so as tempting as the hamburger may look to me at that time, I know there's something better for me if I wait.[8]

Further, it is never too late to begin a lifestyle of single purity. This decision was demonstrated by singer Toni Braxton's decision to reserve sex for marriage: "I've recently decided that I wouldn't be having sex again until I'm married." She added, "A guy might be able to slow me down, but he's not going to break me. Anything that puts me in temptation, I'm resisting."[9]

The challenge of sanctified sex is a supernatural challenge to rise above life's common thrills and reach up for what I call the "realistic ideal." Consider this: Our "ideal" car may be a BMW, Mercedes, Lexus, or even a Rolls Royce. But there's usually just one thing that stands between our "ideal" car and what we are currently driving: money! If we could find a better way to invest and manage our money so that it works for us, then with a few breaks and a lot of hard work, our ideal could be achieved. But the main thing required is discipline.

Whether it is a cruise, a car, or a house, if we want something bad enough we will discipline and deny ourselves today for what we desire tomorrow. As mentioned earlier, this is the concept of "deferred gratification" in action. What we often settle for is immediate gratification. This is the "I can't wait" spirit in operation. Most things that are worthwhile in life involve a wait. Conversely, most things that are free or cheap are immediately available. When we begin to view sexuality from this perspective, our decisions about sex become a matter of whether we will wait for God's best or are willing to settle for much less. God's desire is not to destroy our enjoyment in life but to deepen it.

Rick Stedman proposes a seemingly revolutionary approach to physical interaction between couples who are single. His purpose is to help single couples strengthen values and respect in relationships that are headed toward marriage. Some counselors advise couples to let their level of physical involvement be directly related to their level of commitment. Stedman concurs—to a point. He and the counselors part company at the engagement stage. Even if they abstained from sex while dating, many couples view the engagement stage as being "practically married" and allow their sexual practices to reflect that view. But Stedman points to the tradition of the bride and groom not seeing each other on the day of the wedding. The effect of this practice is to heighten the sense of anticipation and the glory of the moment when the groom sees his bride coming down the aisle. She is usually veiled, which only increases the dramatic allure and excitement of the moment.

This concept of "holding back in order to build up" need not only operate at the wedding ceremony. It can be in effect throughout the relationship. Therefore, instead of increasing the physical and sexual expression during the dating and engagement stages, why not consider decreasing it in order to ensure that the relationship is more "commitment driven" than sex driven?[10]

What a wonderfully radical idea! This approach would assist greatly in clarifying the true essence of relationships.

HOPE AND HELP FOR SEXUAL SIN

Sex can be addictive. In the ideal context of marriage, habit-forming sex is actually healthy, productive, and beneficial to the relationship. But when no commitment is in place, it is sometimes difficult to arrest one's desire for intercourse. The sexual act was designed to be holy and binding, a powerful union of two souls. Therefore, in order to be victorious in overcoming an unhealthy sexual pattern and desire, we must look to God for help. No matter what our sexual history, it is never too late to go to God for forgiveness, healing, and deliverance. With this in mind, let us consider several effective steps to take toward that end.

1. ACKNOWLEDGMENT

Before healing of any kind can occur, we must first admit that a problem exists. For a situation to be brought to light, the blinders of denial and rationalization must first be removed. So, if sex is truly a problem, the first thing to do is to admit it.

2. CONFESSION

Confession means "agreeing with God." Confession basically involves admitting our specific problem to God, and this usually occurs during a private time of meditation and prayer. Confession clears the channel of communication so that healing can occur.

3. REPENTANCE

Genuine repentance is often a lost or forgotten step in the process of successful healing. True repentance involves a deliberate turning away from one thing toward something else. In *Eros Redeemed*, John White captures an intimate glimpse into the heart of repentance: "At times ... repentance will be deep and very, very painful. But the pain will turn into sweet pain, the painful awareness of how greatly I have wounded [God], yet how tenderly in spite of this he loves me."[11] As 2 Corinthians 7:9–10 suggests, the act of repentance undoubtedly brings healing that is effective, goes deep, and endures.

4. CHANGES

Once internal repentance is accomplished, some external alterations will probably be in order. These changes may include avoiding some of the people, places, and circumstances that have contributed to the problem. They may entail even dissolving the relationship if your partner refuses to understand or cooperate.

5. LESSONS

Mistakes become gold mines if we learn crucial lessons from them. A lesson learned is like successfully completing a grade in school. Such lessons need not be repeated in the future. We might even go on to share these lessons with others. Having an accountability partner or group has proved to be effective in encouraging progress and endurance.

6. GUARDIANSHIP

To be sexually on guard does not mean to be relationally paranoid. Rather, it means to be aware of our surroundings and ready to defend our ground if necessary. This kind of readiness is reflected in Ephesians 6:11, which calls us to daily put on the "full armor of God" in order to stand against any temptations that may come our way.

These steps are not intended to become a complicated set of rituals that must be followed precisely in order to receive forgiveness and experience healing. Bishop T. D. Jakes simplifies the whole process in concisely saying, "Admit it, Quit it, and Forget it!"[12]

SOME PRACTICAL TIPS

On a practical note, here are a few tips toward healthy change that I have gathered from my own personal dating experiences:

Begin and end your time together with prayer. When prayer is on both ends of a date, what happens in between will be more honoring to God.

Set standards before you need them. The time to start deciding what you will or will not do is not at 3 A.M. on the sofa or on the carpet in front of the fireplace with the lights low and the music sweet. Write your guidelines on paper and discuss them so that there will be no misunderstanding.

Avoid lateness, darkness, and extended privacy. This trio can team up to make it difficult to maintain standards.

Keep all your clothes on and stay vertical. A horizontal posture tends to increase passion.

Let the strong one help the weak one. There will be times when one partner may be more sexually vulnerable than the other. Both parties have a mutual responsibility to uphold the established standards.

When in doubt, leave it out. If you have an uneasy feeling about some action being contemplated, it is probably best to avoid it altogether.

Regulate the amount and content of media exposure. Radio and television are powerful shapers of our conscious and subconscious selves. We tend to imitate what we hear and what we see, especially when exposed to something repeatedly.

Develop intergender platonic friendships. Every single person needs friends of the other gender with whom to share in a non-romantic, nonsexual manner. Such relationships are valuable in helping us to improve our primary, romantic relationship.

CONCLUSION

Whether single or married, the way we choose to handle our sexuality depends a great deal on how we express the three qualities of love, honor, and respect. How much do we love, honor, and respect ourselves? How much do we love, honor, and respect our partner? And how much do we love, honor, and respect God? When we give honest answers to these questions, we will be able to develop a more reliable understanding of our sexuality and our relationships. Sacrificing sex in order to honor God and ourselves is a way to love and honor our future spouse even before we know who that person will be. And that is what I call "sanctified sex."

LET'S TALK!

1. Read Hebrews 13:4 and 1 Corinthians 7:1–5. What principles found here assist in moving singles toward sanctified sexuality?
2. Do the words *sanctified* and *sex* seem a strange mismatch when placed together? Why or why not?
3. What are some of the factors that cause people to misunderstand the difference between sex as an initiation for a romantic relationship and sex as the consummation of a marriage relationship?
4. What images initially come to mind when you first hear the words *abstinence* and *celibacy*?
5. What criteria do you use to distinguish between a dating partner who is serious and one who is merely curious?
6. Have you ever consciously or unconsciously compared the kisses of different dating partners? Did the comparison have any effect on your attitude? Do you think that sexual comparisons could affect your sex life in marriage?

7. Describe your "realistic ideal" mate.
8. What do you think of the idea of decreasing physical contact as relational commitment increases?
9. Discuss the prospect and possibility of loving your future spouse, before you even know who he or she is, through saving sex for marriage. Are there other ways to accomplish this?

Chapter 5

BEYOND DINNER AND A MOVIE

Creative Ideas for an Above-Average Courtship

ANATOMY OF A TYPICAL DATE

It is Friday night, and after a long week of work, Monique has been looking forward to spending some time with Jamal—that new and special someone in her life. He shows up for their second date at 7:30 in classy casual clothes with the scent of expensive cologne. The high-gloss, spot-free detailing of Jamal's ride is only surpassed by the meticulous application of Monique's make-up and the exquisite tailoring of her outfit. As they exchange approving glances, they both realize they are still in the first-impression stage of the relationship. So the conversation begins:

Jamal: So wassup?
Monique: Nothing much, jus' chillin'.
Jamal: Oh yeah?
Monique: Yeah.
Jamal: You lookin' good, girl.
Monique: (*Nervous laugh*) Aw, I just threw somethin' on.
Jamal: So what you wanna do?
Monique: Anything.
Jamal: (*With arched eyebrows*) *Anything?*
Monique: Well, not *anything!*
Both: (*Laughter*)

Jamal and Monique decide to stop at a restaurant that they happen to see after driving around for several blocks. They browse through the menu and engage in small talk until the meals arrive. Monique had not realized that the Shrimp Pasta would contain so many unruly noodles. Although she has not eaten since before noon, she "plays" with her food because there is just no dainty way to do these noodles. Monique is ever so grateful when Jamal excuses himself to go to the restroom. The noodles disappear in forty seconds flat.

After making up their minds to take in a movie, they leave the restaurant and chat in the car about Jamal's latest CD. At the theater they settle into comfortable seats next to another couple. The previews run, and just before the main feature begins, a group of chatty fifteen-year-olds find seats two rows in front of them. An older man seated directly behind them seems to be recovering from a bad cold. At nine o'clock the action thriller begins.

Two and a half hours later, the movie credits roll and Jamal and Monique emerge from the theater, jump into the car, and discuss the pros and cons of the film. It is now almost midnight as they drive down to "the strip" and hang with the "homeies" for a while. They spend the time chatting and casually watching people who are there to watch other people. Before long, it is almost 1:15 A.M., and Jamal is thinking about the early Saturday morning shift he has to pull at his job. He drives Monique home, and after a couple of car smooches, she walks to her door, waves good-bye, and disappears. It is 1:45 A.M. as Jamal drives toward home and Monique begins to get ready for bed. Their thoughts turn toward each other and to the fact that they have just spent over six hours together, yet they still don't know each other's middle name or favorite color, much less anything about the other's spiritual life or greatest ambition.

How could that happen? Let us look back on this typical date to analyze it and discuss some ways to improve it.

PROBLEM 1: LACK OF PLANNING

Jamal and Monique did not communicate with each other before the date about plans or preferences. Consequently, Jamal decided to wait until they got together that night and just "let the vibes dictate the destination." While this approach might sound suave, it can also lead to a boring time together. Lack of planning is a symptom of laziness, low initiative, and lack of creativity.

Solution 1: Strategic Planning

"Strategic planning" does not suggest a process of robotically choreographing every word and move throughout the dating experience so that all traces of spontaneity are effectively erased. On the contrary, strategic planning can actually provide greater opportunities for "planned spontaneity." In planning your times together you take control of what happens rather than leaving it all to circumstances. (Mr. Circumstances can be a very cruel date manager.) Although the best of strategies sometimes goes awry, it is better to have an altered game plan than to have no game plan at all.

PROBLEM 2: PREDICTABILITY

My survey, mentioned earlier, inquired about the most common activities for a "typical date." Incredibly, 100% of the African-American single adults surveyed identified the very same activity as a typical date: dinner and a movie. When it comes to relationships, the greater the predictability, the greater the "yawnability." If your dating relationship were an oil painting, wouldn't you want to use more than one color? If your dating relationship were a piano score, wouldn't you want to play more than one note? Be assured that your relationship recipe will taste much better with a variety of experiential spices in the mix.

Solution 2: Creativity and Planned Surprise

Males do not have to be the ones to plan every date. Some dates can involve collaboration, and others can be planned entirely by the woman. However, when a date is individually planned, a good approach is to "keep 'em guessing." Even couples who have been married for years fare far better when they refuse to allow their marriage to slip into the rut of routine. Any relationship becomes healthier through our fanning the flame of creativity. Consider the following scenario:

Michelle went on six different dates during the fall semester of her junior year of college. Three of those guys took her to dinner and a movie. Two others were a little more creative and did the movie first, then the dinner. But then she went out with J.T. After picking her up on time and opening the car door for her, he engaged her in substantive conversation as he drove. Unannounced, he pulled into a beautiful and spacious city park at sunset. He stopped the car next to a historic monument with a duck pond and wide grassy spaces nearby. As he got out of the car, his only words were "Wait here."

J.T. opened the trunk, removed a card table along with two folding chairs, and placed them a few yards away on the well-trimmed grass near the monument. He retrieved some other articles from the trunk, and on top of the table placed a white linen tablecloth, two long-stemmed glasses, two lighted candles, a bottle of sparkling grape juice, a small straw basket containing two gourmet sandwiches, and a clear vase with a single rose. As she sat in the car, Michelle's curiosity increased with each passing moment. J.T.'s final touch was a portable stereo softly playing Michelle's favorite saxophone music. As he approached the car with a slight smile on his face, J.T. opened her door in chauffeur style, bowed royally, and extended his outstretched hand toward the inviting table. As they slowly walked hand in hand toward the elegant spread, two other cars with couples rode by—with the women in awe. But of course, these couples could not stop and stare. It would be rude, and besides, that would make them late for their movie.

Michelle had other dates during her college years, but there was only one that she still remembers even ten years later.

(The list starting on page 73 offers a few creative dating ideas to help you get started.)

PROBLEM 3: ANEMIC CONVERSATION

Let's go back to our other couple, Jamal and Monique. There is sometimes a tendency to expect the man to totally carry the conversation especially in the early stages of the relationship. Yet both parties should be active in the communication process. At times conversation flows naturally. But when effort becomes necessary, it should be a joint effort. Anemic conversation centers on subjects of little or no consequence to the couple or to the world. This focus is on things that do not really matter. Small minds discuss weather, people, and events. Great minds discuss feelings, ideas, concepts, and visions.

54 CREATIVE AND CONSTRUCTIVE DATING IDEAS

Damage Control:
   N = No Money
   L = Low Money
   M = Mo' Money
   B = Blow Money

1. Visit a zoo and feed the animals. (N, L)
2. Visit a church and worship together. (L)
3. Walk through the mall and people-watch (and try to guess occupations). (N)
4. Drive to a nearby town for sight-seeing. (N, L)
5. Go for a walk in the moonlight or walk through the park and feed the birds. (N)
6. Go witnessing or do some other ministry activity using your spiritual gifts. (N)
7. Purchase and cook an entire meal or make ice-cream sundaes. (L, M)
8. Go boating, rafting, water skiing, water biking, or canoeing . (L, M)
9. Wash a car (do your own car or surprise a parent or senior citizen). (N)
10. Plant a flower or shrub together and allow it to symbolize your relationship. (L)
11. Fly a kite. (N, L)
12. Create an original poem, song, or dramatic sketch. (N)
13. Create acrostics of each other's names reflecting personality traits. (N)
14. Rake leaves or clean house (for self, parents, or someone with a disability). (N)
15. Do a painting or poster together that reflects your relationship. (N, L)
16. Have an indoor or outdoor picnic with a blanket on the floor or ground. (N, L)
17. Hang out at the airport and watch departures and arrivals of people and planes. (N, L)
18. Use a video camera to create a music video or short movie. (L, M)

19. Visit a hospital or nursing home and encourage someone. (N)
20. Walk through a cemetery (daytime only!) and read the markers. (N)
21. Have a joint Bible study on a specific topic. (N)
22. Visit a library or museum and research a mutually interesting topic. (N)
23. Paint her fingernails or restyle his or her hair. (N)
24. Go bowling or play tennis or another sport. (N, L)
25. Play "Ask Me Anything" or the Ungame; discuss goals, plans, likes, and dislikes. (N)
26. Have a personal talent show. (N)
27. Look through a family photo album together and discuss the term *relationship* with your parents. (N)
28. Go on a double date with your parents. (L, M)
29. Buy a bottle of Superbubbles, go to a high area, and blow bubbles down. (L)
30. Pray with and for each other at the beginning and end of your date and conduct a spiritual fast together. (N)
31. Go fishing. (L, M)
32. Rent a limousine and tour the town. (B)
33. Go car shopping (even if it's just window shopping). (N)
34. Take a ride in a horse-drawn carriage. (M)
35. Be baby-sitters for a couple so they can go on a date. (N)
36. Take a tour of "open houses" of homes for sale and discuss what you like and dislike about them. (N)
37. Design an elaborate treasure hunt with several clues and messages that eventually lead your partner across the city to a posh restaurant where you're waiting at an intimate table for two. (M, B)
38. Arrange for a musician to serenade you and your companion at a restaurant or in a park. (N, L, M)
39. Take a class together to learn a new subject, then study together. (L, M)
40. Get together early on Saturday morning and visit garage/yard sales. (N, L)

41. Visit an auction just to watch or perhaps to participate in the lower bidding process. (N, L)

42. Take a tour of antique shops in your town. (N)

43. Go to an exclusive hotel lobby to sit down and people-watch. (N)

44. Attend a singles conference together. (L, M)

45. Ride bicycles. (N, L)

46. Get a camera, find a nice location, and become a "Model for a Day." (L) Option: Take turns posing for the funniest, most dramatic, or most original shot.

47. Do a joint short-term business venture. Split the profits or establish a savings fund for future dates. (M)

48. Attend a wedding together. (N, L)

49. Volunteer to serve the homeless at a local shelter. (N)

50. Volunteer at a juvenile home, a jail, or a prison. (N)

51. Go snow sledding or skiing, or build a snow family. (N, L, M)

52. Dress up in rented costumes or other outrageous clothing (e.g., wigs, glasses) and take a walk through the mall. (N, L, M)

53. Take a ride in a hot-air balloon, helicopter, or chartered private plane. (B)

54. Write a description of five complete date options on 3 x 5 index cards. Allow your date to pick one without knowing what is on each card. (M) Option: Allow him or her to choose another card as a substitution if he or she desires to take the chance.

Solution 3: Creative Conversation

Since time is so valuable, why not talk about things that really matter in life? This entails going beyond the ordinary brand of bland chatter. Small minds make small talk. Creative conversation involves substantive speaking, unusual questions, and intentional listening. Although this may initially require some extra personal effort, with practice it will evolve into a healthy habit with valuable benefits.

Because communication is such an important subject, we suggest several categories of uncommon questions and conversation starters that reflect many different levels of relationship maturity. We should be thoughtful and discreet as to which questions are appropriate for which relationships. If you try these questions and dating ideas, we guarantee two outcomes: (1) You will get to know a great deal more about yourself and your partner in using creative conversation, and (2) through creative dating you will have many significant and unusual experiences that neither you nor your partner will forget.

(Several additional conversation starters may be found in the appendix.)

LET'S TALK!

1. How does Colossians 3:17, 23–24 relate to the subject of creative dating and substantive conversation?
2. What is a typical date for you?
3. Discuss the pros and cons of Jamal and Monique's date. What was good, and what needs to be improved? What letter grade would you give their date?
4. What was the basic difference in J.T.'s approach in his date with Michelle as compared with Jamal and Monique?
5. What are some ways to detect a person's character early in a dating relationship?
6. Which is your favorite and your least favorite of the dating ideas featured in this chapter?
7. Describe the most creative date you have ever planned or experienced?
8. Use the first letter of your last name and discuss the questions that correspond to that letter in the list of creative conversation starters.

CREATIVE CONVERSATION

From A to Z ... and then some!

A. Family Matters

1. What are your earliest memories of growing up?
2. Describe the relationship between your parents. Would you want a similar relationship?
3. What were some spoken or unspoken rules within your family?
4. What trend in your family makes you proud? What trend makes you sad or angry?
5. Who is your favorite relative? Tell why.

B. What's God Got to Do with It?

1. What do you think God thinks about you?
2. What do you think of Jesus?
3. How often do you pray and/or read the Bible?
4. Name a favorite Bible story or character and explain why you like that one.
5. Do you have a spiritual gift? If so, in what ways do you use it?

C. The Mind and Intellect

1. What are some of your favorite books?
2. Are you computer literate? Do you surf the Net, have a home page, or receive e mail?
3. Whom do you admire for his or her wisdom or intellect?
4. Do your have a favorite quote or saying that helps to guide your life?
5. If you had to write a book about your life, what would be the title?

D. So Very Social

1. Who is your best friend (besides me, of course)? What do you like most about this person?
2. Do you consider yourself an introvert or an extrovert? Why?
3. You are stranded on a remote island for a year. Name the three things you'd most want to have with you.
4. Do you feel that most people are basically bad or basically good? Why?

5.   Suppose you were given one wish to change the world. What would it be?

E. Let's Get Physical

1.   How do you feel about regular exercise?
2.   How much attention do you pay to the kinds of food you eat?
3.   How do you feel about drinking alcohol?
4.   How do you feel about smoking?
5.   Have you ever experimented with marijuana, crack, or other drugs?

F. Heart and Goal

1.   How would you want your obituary to read?
2.   Do you maintain a daily to-do list?
3.   What would you like to accomplish within the next five years?
4.   How will your life be different in the next ten years?
5.   What is it that you want to accomplish before dying?

G. What a Character!

1.   How do you determine right from wrong?
2.   Name some life principles you absolutely refuse to compromise.
3.   What in life do you value the most?
4.   What controversial subjects do you have strong feelings about?
5.   In what situations do you reflect a public self and a private self?

H. Personality Plus

1.   Describe your personality in one word.
2.   Would you say your primary personality is cold, cool, warm, or hot? Explain.
3.   Is there any aspect of your personality that you wish you could change?
4.   Describe your moods and what triggers them?
5.   If you could be the clone of any famous person, who would it be, and why?

I. Show Me the Money

1.   Which word best describes you: spender, saver, or investor?

2. You have just been given $100,000 that you must use in one month. What will you do with it?
3. Did you get an allowance when you were growing up? At what age did it begin?
4. What kind of car would you like most if you had the money, and why?
5. Do you keep a budget or a record of how you spend your money?

J. It's a Black Thing

1. How do you feel about your race and heritage?
2. Do you feel responsible for contributing to the progress of your people?
3. In what ways do you give back to your community?
4. Name a famous Black figure of the past or present whom you admire. Explain why you do.
5. In terms of racism, how was life different for your parents as they were growing up than it was for you?

K. Gender Mender

1. What is your attitude toward men/women in general?
2. What are the usual conflicts you have with men/women?
3. What do you like best about men/women?
4. What attracts you most in a man /woman?
5. What repels you in a man/woman?

L. Great Expectations

1. If you spend a lot of money on a date, do you expect physical closeness in return?
2. What do you want most from a date?
3. Do you expect a little or a lot from others? From yourself?
4. What or where would you like to be ten years from now?
5. How do you react when your expectations are unfulfilled?

M. Trust Me

1. Is it ever okay to lie or stretch the truth? Under what circumstances?

2. Would you tell someone something you knew they wanted to hear even though it was not actually the way you felt?

3. Would you say you are honest sometimes, most times, or all of the time?

4. How do you feel about developing more than one relationship at a time?'

5. If you could save someone's life by telling a lie, would you do it?

N. Your Image of You

1. If you compared yourself to a vehicle or animal, what kind would you be? Why?

2. What is your favorite part of your face?

3. If you could change something about yourself, what would it be?

4. If you were placed in a singles auction, who would bid on you, and how much would you bring?

5. How would you describe yourself in a personal newspaper advertisement?

O. Your Image of Me

1. To what kind of vehicle or animal would you compare me? Why?

2. What is your favorite part of my face?

3. If you could change something about me, what would it be?

4. Who would play you in a movie?

5. If you had to introduce me, let's say as a speaker before a large audience, what would you say?

P. The Power of Purpose

1. Why were you born?

2. What is your purpose in life?

3. Would you be willing to risk your life to save someone else?

4. What is your biggest dream?

5. What one thing would you like most to accomplish in your life?

Q. R-E-S-P-E-C-T

1. What does it mean to respect yourself and others?

2. What do you like most about yourself? Least?

3. What do you like most about me? Least?

4. How do you feel when someone treats you disrespectfully? How do you respond?

5. What do you respect most about your father/mother?

R. My Favorite Things

1. My favorite color is _____. Why?

2. My favorite song is _____. Why?

3. My favorite food is _____. Why?

4. My favorite pastime is _____. Why?

5. My favorite person is _____. Why?

S. Second that Emotion

1. What makes you angry, and why?

2. What makes you afraid, and why?

3. What makes you laugh, and why?

4. What makes you sad, and why?

5. What makes you thankful, and why?

T. Nothing Like Experience

1. Tell me about your most embarrassing experience.

2. Tell me about your most exciting experience.

3. Tell me about your most dangerous or frightening experience.

4. Tell me about your most pleasant or fulfilling experience.

5. Tell me about your most worshipful experience.

U. Uniqueness

1. Name one unique thing about yourself.

2. Name one unique thing about me.

3. Name one unique thing about us.

4. What does it mean to treat (or to be treated) special?

5. Is special treatment important to you? Why or why not?

V. Romance Me

1. What is your concept of romance?

2. Is romance important to you? Why or why not?

3. Would you rather be treated to a surprise romantic occasion, or to a known and planned romantic occasion that you could look forward to?
4. Describe your ideal romantic dream.
5. What makes romance last?

W. Love Unconditional
1. What does the word *love* mean to you?
2. How do you communicate love?
3. What drives or motivates your love?
4. Compare and contrast your view of love with the following: infatuation, friendship, and lust.
5. Do you see any necessary connection between love and God? Explain.

X. Generation Sex
1. Describe what is sexually attractive to you.
2. What is the purpose of sex?
3. For you, what determines if and when sex is appropriate?
4. If your best friend or roommate told you he/she was still a virgin at age twenty-one, how would you respond?
5. What are your feelings about reserving sex for marriage?

Y. With This Ring
1. How do you know when someone is the right one for you?
2. What are your expectations of a partner in marriage?
3. What would make you want to file for divorce?
4. Do you want to have children? If so, how many?
5. What role, if any, does God play in a marriage?

Z. The Five Senses
1. Which one of the five senses is the most valuable to you and why?
2. What kinds of sights bring you the most joy?
3. What sounds and smells remind you of home?
4. What is your favorite kind of food?
5. How do you feel when you touch a baby?

Chapter 6

COMMON QUESTIONS, UNCOMMON ANSWERS

20 Things You've Always Wondered About But Never Asked

The subject of male-female relationships covers such a wide range of topics that no single book could adequately address every individual question or concern. However, there is one book that contains overarching principles that can be applied to practically every life experience imaginable. This book is the Bible. Although written many years ago, the words of the Bible are words of life and remain relevant even in the twenty-first century.

The answers provided in this chapter encompass a biblical perspective as a foundation combined with personal and practical experience. But be aware that many of the responses are not the normal, average, regular, common, typical answers and they could be hazardous to your usual way of thinking. These responses frequently go beyond the typical perspective to address areas of concern.

QUESTION #1: WHERE ARE ALL THE GOOD MEN?

BIBLICAL FOCUS: 1 TIMOTHY 6:11–14

People offer a variety of definitions of what constitutes a "good" man. Some base goodness on physical traits and financial marketability while others appreciate more character-based personal components such as commitment and patience. During my research for this book, several sisters listed the traits they desire in a partner as romance, honesty, trustworthiness, and spirituality. Truly, all of these are important. But let's look at goodness from a spiritual perspective, using 1 Timothy 6:11–14 as our starting point. According to this passage, a "good man" is—

Righteous: He conducts life from God's perspective with honesty and justice for all.

Godly: His ways imitate God's ways as he seeks to reflect God's character.

Filled with faith: He is willing to step out and trust beyond the unknown and unseen.

Loving: He expresses unselfish, unconditional commitment.

Steady: He is consistent despite changing or fluctuating conditions.

Gentle: He is sensitive to the needs and feelings of others.

Christian: He is a recipient of the promises and benefits of those who have surrendered to Jesus Christ.

Active in public worship: He freely worships God in public and is unashamed of his faith.

Active in private worship: He regularly spends time alone with God.

Obedient: He keeps God's commandments without frequent wavering.

Now that we have established what a good man is, where can one be found? Whether it be a good man or a good woman, the place to find him or her is *not* in a club or singles bar. One cannot go fishing in a swamp and expect to catch rainbow trout. Most fishermen or women who choose to fish in a swamp usually reel in a creature of the swamp. The chances of encountering a positive potential partner are significantly increased through simply excelling in what comes most naturally to you. There is no need, for example, to take up racquetball just to meet people—especially if you hate the sport. Great places for interacting with other positive singles include church singles' retreats and conferences, the library, the grocery store, church (your own or another), work, weddings, other people's family reunions, plays, health clubs, and college classes.[1]

QUESTION #2: WHERE ARE ALL THE GOOD WOMEN?

BIBLICAL FOCUS: PROVERBS 31:10 - 31

There *are* men out there who are searching for good women. Commonly speaking, most men tend to identify a "good" woman as one who is physically attractive, shows respect, displays a sense of humor, and exhibits a vibrant personality. Beyond these desirable traits, however, Proverbs 31 offers the following characteristics that reflect a woman of excellence:

Trustworthy: She demonstrates dependability.

Thoughtful: She rejects evil and embraces goodness.

Industrious: She is not lazy; she takes care of herself and others.

Business minded: She is wise and practical regarding business matters.

Physically fit: She keeps her body healthy and toned.

Caring: She helps those in need.

Organized: She thinks and plans ahead.

Well dressed: She dresses attractively.

Strong and dignified: She has self-confidence and carries herself gracefully.

Wise and kind: She is well spoken, expressing encouragement and good judgment.

Godly: She respects and obeys God.

QUESTION #3: HOW FAR IS TOO FAR IN PHYSICALLY EXPRESSING AFFECTION?

BIBLICAL FOCUS: 1 THESSALONIANS 4:2 - 8

This question seems to be based on the assumption that the farther one can go in the regard to physical expression, the better. However, we must understand that in a normal relationship, physical or sexual expression is progressive, and therefore the more one experiences, the greater becomes the desire. If one desires to develop a healthy and balanced relationship, a better question might be, "How far away is far enough in order to keep the more important qualities in proper perspective?"

Each partner must know the other's limits, particularly when they are committed to reserving sexual intercourse for marriage. An activity that is tolerable for one may be unbearable for the other. Two suggestions: (1) Review the Practical Tips given at the end of chapter 4, and (2) consider reading Ray Short's great little book *Sex, Love or Infatuation?*[22]

There are two personal signals that can help you determine when one has gone too far in the sexual arena:

> **The Spiritual/Psychological Indicator.** Our conscience or inner voice is often an accurate indicator of when something is not right. It would be wise to develop a practice of listening to this voice, which will flash "amber lights" into our spirit or conscience to warn us of impending danger. The problem is that we often ignore our misgivings and cover them with compromise and rationalizations.
>
> **The Physical/Sexual Indicator.** Every normally functioning human body, whether male or female, has built-in physical indicators of how far is too far. The alarm goes off when the body begins to physically prepare itself for sex. This is one unmistakable indicator of "too far."

QUESTION #4: IS IT OKAY TO DATE OR MARRY INTERRACIALLY?

BIBLICAL FOCUS: NUMBERS 12:1-11

Interracial romantic relationships have long been a point of controversy, particularly in the United States because of the nation's history in race relations. Yet the choice of whom to date and marry is a matter of personal freedom and preference. There is no biblical mandate forbidding interracial relationships. Of course, no relationship should be entered blindly. Interracial couples should be prepared for the social stigmatization and backlash that may be created by such unions. A marriage between persons of the same race intrinsically carries its own set of challenges, but extra daily stress and pressures will indubitably apply to a relationship that is interracial. This pressure extends from the couple to in-laws, friendships, business associates, and even strangers in the mall. Interracial couples might well follow the Boy Scouts' motto: "Be Prepared!"

QUESTION #5: HOW CAN I TACTFULLY RESPOND TO UNWANTED SEXUAL PRESSURE IN A RELATIONSHIP?

BIBLICAL FOCUS: 1 CORINTHIANS 6:12 – 20

The first thing is to become secure enough within yourself that you know exactly what you want in life and are not willing to compromise certain personal principles regardless of the protests and pressure applied by others. Once you have clearly established your sexual boundaries and parameters, and your partner seeks to push you beyond these limits, then you know that person does not respect you anyway. At that point, you have the option of trying to honestly explain to the person how disrespected you feel. If the person listens and understands, the two of you can agree on certain consequences if the pressure is asserted again. If you detect a pattern, it may be best to leave the relationship.

QUESTION #6: AS A SINGLE PERSON, HOW CAN I RESPONSIBLY DEAL WITH MY SEXUAL URGES?

BIBLICAL FOCUS: 1 CORINTHIANS 10:12 – 13

As noted earlier, the most important sexual organ is the mind. The mind must be conditioned and developed to cooperate with your will. There are many different sources of sexual stimuli. The flesh is usually a very greedy animal: the more it consumes, the more it desires. Therefore the key to control is in the level of intake. Discipline is the name of the game here. It doesn't help to deny your feelings. If feelings are submerged rather than dealt with, they will likely resurface in an unexpected and undesirable manner. Sexual energy can be positively channeled through individual or joint activities such as athletics, creative writing, or helping someone in need.

QUESTION #7: WHAT ABOUT DATING OR MARRYING SOMEONE WHO IS OF A DIFFERENT FAITH OR HAS NO RELATIONSHIP WITH GOD?

BIBLICAL FOCUS: 2 CORINTHIANS 6:14 – 17

One important consideration is the degree of difference between the two approaches to God. Is the difference primarily concentrated in the style of the faith, or are there radically fundamental differences? A way to discover this is to examine both written statements of faith. Write down separately what you individually consider the primary tenets or "nonnegotiables" of your respective faiths. Is one willing to tolerate and even celebrate the faith of the other? If not, trouble could be lurking. Some couples have adopted a third faith that represents a compromise between the other two. Be wary of any denomination that has absolutely no room for any variation in practice or teaching. From a Christian perspective, a good question to ask is "Who is Jesus?" Jesus must be regarded as God in the flesh in order for a faith to be truly Christian.

Other difficulties can occur if one partner embraces faith in God and the other does not. The faith factor is often a foundational element that can produce relational discord when partners are not in spiritual harmony. Here are some practical observations on the matter:

—It is unwise to date someone with the idea of changing or reforming him or her later. What you see is usually what you get.

—If there is any changing to be done, it may well be the person with faith who experiences a weakening or loss of faith.

—Just as it makes no sense to begin a cross-country trip with a slow leak or a flat tire, it is similarly unwise to begin a relationship journey with a faith deficiency.

—Some may say, "I know of a couple who started out spiritually mismatched, but later they developed a harmonious relationship." To this I say there was a couple who decided to swim for six hours in frigid, shark-infested waters and were not drowned, attacked, or frozen to death. They made it safely to shore. Now we must decide whether living dangerously should be the exception or the norm.

QUESTION #8: IS THERE ANY HOPE FOR ME AS A SINGLE PARENT?

BIBLICAL FOCUS: ISAIAH 54:4-8

The issues involved in single parenthood are many, ranging from divorce (willing or unwilling), adoption, bereavement, and extended family. Regardless of how it occurs, single parenthood offers a true challenge to one's endurance, especially when the little darlings have worked your last nerves. Two perspectives should be kept in mind. The first is the children's perspective. In most cases the children are not the cause of one's problems. A child needs not only the parent's attention and affection but also sufficient exposure to positive role models of the other gender. Just as male and female are involved in creating a child, so males and females should be involved in the child's nurture and development.

The second perspective involves the single parent. If you do not take some time for yourself, how will you have anything to give to someone else? It is easy to lose yourself in caring for your child, so you must deliberately schedule time for yourself. Visit friends, explore new interests, continue to grow and learn, and even pamper yourself. In her book *Single Principles,* Sheron Patterson provides precious insight into the single-parenting situation:

> Single parenting is like a tightrope you walk while carrying the weight of the world on your shoulders before a tremendous audience. Some of the spectators are rooting for you to make it. Others want you to fall. Either way, though, the audience is little help. You have to believe in yourself. On the tightrope, high levels of self-esteem and self-love will provide balance. Accepting your single parenthood will keep you walking. And strong faith in God will let you strut. . . .[3]

QUESTION #9: HOW CAN I HANDLE DATING AFTER A DIVORCE OR WIDOWHOOD OR ALONG WITH SINGLE PARENTHOOD?

BIBLICAL FOCUS: RUTH 1 - 4; ACTS 16:13 - 15

Much depends on the circumstances of the divorce or the single-parent situation. A divorce that involves children is obviously a more complicated situation than one without children. Most divorces are unnecessary. Even those that seem inevitable should not be bitter or vindictive, especially when children are involved. It makes no sense, for example, to complain to your children about your "ex" whether he or she is present or absent. Such talk may make one parent feel better temporarily, but it can leave deep scars in a child's emotional psyche.

For a parent to date a person who is a stranger to the children can be traumatic if the matter is not approached with utmost care. In the early stages of dating it would be good to meet the person somewhere other than the home. This is more important when dating several people, in order to avoid exposing the child to too many different personalities too soon. Each dating partner can prompt a sense of invasion and the kind of stress that typically comes with a significant change. If, after talking to your child about your dating partner, you sense that your child may be ready to meet him or her, this meeting could occur within a larger group setting in order to reduce the stress levels of all parties involved. If this initial encounter goes well, the rest of the journey should include frequent and open communication. Most importantly, proceed with caution.

QUESTION #10: SHOULD WOMEN TAKE THE INITIATIVE TO PURSUE ROMANTIC RELATIONSHIPS?

BIBLICAL FOCUS: PROVERBS 18:22

Of course, the "old school" of thought holds that women should never pursue men, whereas the "new school" allows for anyone to initiate a relationship. There is some truth and wisdom in both approaches. Since many men hold little respect for women who have a tendency to chase men, this may not be a good idea. However, there is a vast difference between initiating a romance and initiating a friend-ship. Because men are so goal-oriented, when a woman "demands" a man, she "de-mans" that man. But when a woman befriends a man, she gains a friend in that man. If a woman truly desires a friendship with a man and the relationship does not progress beyond the friendship level, you may not have gained a romance, but you have gained a friend.

QUESTION #11: WHAT CAN I DO WHEN MY FRIEND WANTS TO BE MORE THAN A FRIEND?

BIBLICAL FOCUS: 1 TIMOTHY 5:2; 2 SAMUEL 13:1–22; 1 CORINTHIANS 7:36–38

Sometimes singles have friendships that they want to keep as friendships, with no romance or dating strings attached. But friend-ships can involve a current of unspoken feelings and uncommunicated assumptions. Sometimes there is mutual agreement for a friendship to turn into romance. But when only one person's imagination takes over, the other person's gestures of friendship are mistaken as gestures of romance. If this pattern continues, it can breed resentment on both sides. The remedy? There must be open, honest communication coupled with a willingness to respect the position of the person who wishes to remain friends. Be aware that the disclosure of a growing romantic affection may cause a great strain in the friendship—even to the point of ending it altogether. Christian singles should remember that sometimes when people think they are attracted to us, they are really attracted to the Christ "in" us.[4] When this occurs and we only offer them ourselves, they end up tremendously short-changed.

QUESTION #12: HOW DO I HANDLE A LONG DATING RELATIONSHIP IF THERE IS STILL NO EVIDENCE OF A DESIRE FOR COMMITMENT?

BIBLICAL FOCUS: GENESIS 29:16–26

For many people, the "C" word represents a very scary thought. Our past may include an absent father, divorced parents, or broken promises in romantic relationships. Such experiences can deeply wound and inhibit us in our willingness to risk vulnerability and commitment in the future. However, just because we have been hurt and disappointed in the past is not a reason to penalize every other partner in the future. Real relationships cannot grow without risk and commitment.

A different aspect of this failure to commit is reflected in the person who desires the benefits and conveniences of commitment without paying the price. Such a person is both lazy and selfish with regard to relationships. The other partner should take a long, hard realistic look at reality and decide whether or not he or she wants to invest valuable time and energy in a relationship without a commitment for the future.

QUESTION #13: IS IT OKAY TO LIVE TOGETHER FOR A WHILE PRIOR TO MARRIAGE?

BIBLICAL FOCUS: HEBREWS 13:4

I will answer this question and then ask one of my own. Surveys have revealed that couples who live together before marriage have a significantly higher percentage of divorces than those who do not live together. Some rationalize the decision to live together in the following ways:

—A piece of paper does not make a marriage anyway.

Response: Most major decisions in life involve commitment and legal sanction. To purchase a house or a car, to adopt a child, to fish or hunt or even own a dog, we must obtain a license or complete other legal procedures. Few complain about these requirements, yet some people balk when it comes to marriage. It makes one wonder where the true priorities lie.

—Living together gives our relationship a "trial period" to see if we are compatible.

Response: The "trial period" prior to marriage is typically the period of engagement. If this stage is developed properly through significant communication, counseling, and prayer, there is no need for living together. Granted, there may be some traits about a person that can only be learned through experience in a domestic situation. However, the key is not to know everything there is to know about a person—that is impossible anyway. The key is to be committed enough to that person so that even if we discover something we don't like, our love and care continue.

—*Living together lets us reduce our bills and save some money for the wedding, honeymoon, a house, or other marriage expenses.*

Response: Saving money is an excellent idea. The engagement period is a great time to develop the discipline of saving and investing. This may mean waiting a little longer for the wedding or having a less expensive wedding, but the discipline involved represents an investment in the relationship itself.

There is another question: **Is it Permissible to Live Together for a While Prior to Marriage?**

Biblically, it is not. The Bible clearly indicates that the sexual relationship is to be reserved for marriage. Marriage is set forth both biblically and historically as the rite of initiation for sexual intercourse and the environment for the most intimate of human relationships. There are numerous injunctions against having sexual relations apart from marriage, including the seventh commandment (Ex. 20:14; Deut. 5:18) and the tenth commandment (Ex. 20:17; Deut. 5:21).

Some people may protest that living together does not mean they are having sexual relations, but the fact remains that living together entails an intimacy that is to be reserved for marriage. A biblical marriage exists not only in the letter of the law but in spirit.

QUESTION #14: WHAT IF WE GET MARRIED AND DISCOVER THAT WE ARE SEXUALLY INCOMPATIBLE?

BIBLICAL FOCUS: SONG OF SONGS 4:1-15; 5:10-16

Sexual satisfaction involves the mind, the desire, and a mutual willingness to make it work. If there are physical or emotional factors that inhibit satisfactory intercourse, there are resources available, physical exercises, and books, all of which can help a couple work through and overcome these obstacles.

QUESTION #15: IS THERE ONLY ONE SPECIAL PERSON IN THE WORLD OUT THERE FOR ME?

BIBLICAL FOCUS: EPHESIANS 3:20

First of all, there are more available women in the world than available men. The reasons for this are males' lower birth rate, shorter life expectancy, prison population, military service, and gay lifestyle. This reality, however, should not cause one to lose hope.

In addition, from a spiritual point of view, a prospective marriage partner could fit into at least three categories:

—Outside God's will (a divine veto here)
—Within God's permissive will (you may select within this range of choices)
—God's specific will (only this one will do)

Concerning mate choice, most fall within the second category.

When it comes to something as serious as a life partner, we must obviously take extreme care to make the right decision. (See chapter 11 for a fuller treatment of this subject.)

QUESTION #16: HOW CAN I KNOW IF I HAVE THE GIFT OF LIFETIME CELIBACY?

BIBLICAL FOCUS: MATTHEW 19:11–12; 1 CORINTHIANS 7:9

The commitment and sacrifice of lifelong celibacy can be a beautiful and powerful expression of spiritual surrender and personal discipline. However, this lifestyle runs directly counter to the norms of contemporary society and has thus earned an undeserved reputation as being undesirable. You can determine in part whether you possess this special gift through your own inner thoughts and desires. Do you often imagine yourself married? Do you long for the constant companionship of a soul mate of the other gender? Do you have a strong desire for sexual union or for starting a family of your own? If your answer to most of these questions is yes, then you probably do not have the gift of celibacy.

By contrast, do you feel comfortable, content, natural, and satisfied with the notion of living the rest of your life without a spouse? Are you able mentally and psychologically to handle solitude? Do you actually enjoy flying solo and feel you can accomplish more by remaining single? If you answered yes to most of these questions, you possibly have the gift of celibacy. It must be understood that just because you do not seem to have the gift of celibacy is no guarantee that you will eventually marry. When it comes to male-female relationships, there are few "guarantees" in this life. This is one of many good reasons to place your faith in God's plan rather than in a woman or a man.

QUESTION #17: AM I STILL A VIRGIN IF I HAVE EXPERIENCED ORAL SEX OR RAPE OR EVEN HAVE GIVEN BIRTH BY ARTIFICIAL INSEMINATION?

BIBLICAL FOCUS: DEUTERONOMY 22:23 – 27; MATTHEW 1:23 – 25

Even though each of these issues requires a distinct answer, one universal statement applies to all: Generally speaking, a virgin is one who has never participated in sexual intercourse. Some people define that term narrowly as meaning only complete penile-vaginal penetration. Moreover, in the past, virginity among women has sometimes been equated with the presence of an intact hymen—a condition that modern sports and other activity might innocently alter. Others consider a person who has been an unwilling victim of sexual penetration still to be a virgin on the technical grounds that true intercourse involves two willing partners. On that basis a victim of heterosexual or homosexual rape or sexual abuse would be regarded as still a virgin.

Beyond the physical or technical perspectives, however, lies the realization that the intimacy of true intercourse also involves the mind, emotions, and spirit. Therefore intercourse and virginity should not be too narrowly defined. Stating the forementioned boundaries is not intended to imply that any premarital sexual activity is okay as long as one remains a technical virgin. We must move beyond the shortsighted notion of "How much can I get away with and remain a virgin?" If physical virginity has already been lost, a state of "secondary virginity," or "spiritual virginity," can be attained through confession, repentance, and a commitment to obey God in sexual matters.

QUESTION #18: HOW CAN I BREAK THE CYCLE OF GIVING IN TO TEMPTATION?

BIBLICAL FOCUS: GALATIANS 5:16–18; 1 CORINTHIANS 10:13; 1 JOHN 4:4

No one is exempt from temptation in its wide variety of forms. However, there are some inner resources and alternative resources we can summon to assist us in this very winnable war.

—Realize that morality and salvation are not vaccinations against temptation. There is no known vaccine that produces immunity to temptation.

—Temptation usually involves a personal choice. Temptation and sin are not synonymous, and just because we are tempted does not mean we must yield. We must decide inside that enough is enough.

—If we intend to win the war of temptation, personal discipline is the name of the game. This must not be a momentary decision, but an ongoing lifestyle.

—Eliminate unnecessary contributors to your temptation, including people, places, and activities that leave you vulnerable.

—Ask a trusted friend to hold you accountable.

—Embrace the power of God, which ultimately is greater than any temptation.

QUESTION #19: HOW CAN I KNOW IF A DATING PARTNER IS REALLY SERIOUS ABOUT THE RELATIONSHIP?

BIBLICAL FOCUS: HEBREWS 4:12

A troublesome relational dilemma can quickly arise when one party in the relationship is on a different timetable for marriage than the other. An open, honest disclosure of the true inner thoughts, feelings, and intentions of both partners is indispensable in such cases. If for some reason you suspect that your partner is being less than totally truthful with you, or if you are personally unsure about the right directions for the future, try the following: Ask God to show you three things:

A. *Ask God to show you your own heart.* The human psyche is quite capable of creating idyllic scenarios that delude us into thinking that something or someone is just right for us when the exact opposite is the case. Therefore it is essential that we get honest enough with God to ask for the truth about our own motives and be prepared to accept the answer.

B. *Ask God to show you your partner's heart.* Whether intentionally or unintentionally, partners sometimes speak words that are untrue and initiate actions that are misleading. But according to Hebrews 4:12, God's Word and God's Spirit can discern the thoughts and intents of the heart. Therefore we should use God's powerful resources even in the social situations of life.

C. *Ask God to show you God's own heart.* It is sad but true that we seldom seek God concerning romantic matters of the heart. In Matthew 7:7–11 Jesus expresses God's desire to give good things to those who ask, seek, and knock. Although God's will may seem shrouded at times, as we acknowledge God in all things, God promises to direct our paths (Proverbs 3:5–6).

QUESTION #20: HOW MUCH RISK, VULNERABILTY, AND UNCONDITIONAL LOVE SHOULD BE INVOLVED IN A DATING RELATIONSHIP AS COMPARED WITH A MARRIAGE?

BIBLICAL FOCUS: MATTHEW 10:16

All Christians are called to love each other with God's kind of love. However, the introduction of the romantic element significantly alters the framework of male-female relationships. Thus, because of the additional emotional baggage accompanying such unions, it is important to properly pace the degree of risk, vulnerability, and unconditional love expressed. One way to accomplish this is to allow one's level of vulnerability to rise no higher than the corresponding level of commitment. The *relationship progression* below may help to clarify this concept.

1. Strangers
2. Informal Acquaintances
3. Acquaintances
4. Associates
5. Casual Friendship   Casual Dating Relationship
6. Close Friendship   Exclusive Dating Relationship
7. Intimate Friendship   Intensive Dating Relationship
8. Pre-Engagement
9. Engagement
10. Marriage

Numbers 5 through 7 reflect various levels of friendship on the left and the corresponding levels of dating relationship on the right. It is easy for problems to emerge if complete vulnerability is expressed so early in the relationship (such as at level 6) that there is nothing left to express in later levels. Another consideration is the need for a safety net of commitment in the event that a relationship accidentally falls from the high wire of dating.

LET'S TALK!

1. Choose the five questions from this chapter that are of greatest interest to you or your singles group.
2. Are there any answers of mine with which you disagree? Explain your response.
3. What questions would you add to this list?
4. Would you ever ask God any of these questions through prayer? Explain.
5. Are some of these subjects often avoided and if so, why? Why do they make people uncomfortable?
6. Did your initial opinions on any of these subjects change after reviewing the Biblical Focus Scriptures?

Chapter 7

SOLO SEX

A Direct Perspective on Masturbation

The next three chapters address the three sexually related topics that are perhaps the most avoided in discourse among singles: masturbation, date rape, and homosexuality. There are just some things that are not to be discussed in polite conversation, right? Maybe not. Whether the conversation is polite or impolite, these matters must be addressed. When issues are intentionally or unintentionally pushed beneath the surface of open communication, this gives more power to the problem. But when they are openly discussed, this process supplies more power to the people. Although there may not be universal agreement at every point, at least some questions can be raised, and the dialogue can begin.

Perhaps the most challenging, least discussed, most practiced, and least understood subject among singles today is masturbation. Although research figures vary concerning the frequency of masturbation, most sources estimate that 50–60% of females and more than 90% of males have masturbated at some point in their lives. Perhaps the reason that the figure for males is so much higher is that men are more physically connected to their sexuality, whereas women tend to be more emotionally wired.[1] Some sources contend that due to this difference, females must "learn" masturbation. Yet, once awakened, this practice can become even more controlling than for a man. In the comprehensive national sex survey published as *Sex in America*, the researchers discovered that the most frequent reason given for masturbation was "to relieve sexual tension." The second reason was the lack of an available sexual partner.[2] Some sources contend that much of the perceived sexual pressure experienced by people who practice masturbation is less internally and more externally induced by America's sexually charged society.[3]

If masturbation is so widely practiced, why is it so seldom discussed openly? A very likely cause is the guilt associated with the practice. In the *Sex in America* national survey, of the men surveyed who masturbated once a week or more, 41% said they experienced some level of guilt. Of the women who practiced self-stimulation one to five times per year, 47% said they felt guilty to some degree ranging from "rarely" to "always."[4] How can such a private, personal practice produce such a high frequency of guilt feelings? We may discover the answer as we consider common myths and misconceptions of masturbation.

MYTHS AND MISCONCEPTIONS

The very mention of the word *masturbation* conjures up Victorian images of a secrecy-shrouded, clandestine act certain to lead to any variety of diseases, debilitations, and mental malfunctions. In the mid-nineteenth century many Americans were obsessed with the idea that masturbation was dangerous and evil. Two businessmen capitalized on this fear and suggested that their product was the answer. J. H. Kellogg (as in cornflakes) and Sylvester Graham (as in graham crackers) independently of each other suggested that their foods would assist in quelling the urge to masturbate. Both men wrote best-selling books that mentioned masturbation. Graham's 1834 book was entitled *A Lecture to a Young Man*, and Kellogg's 1888 work was called *Plain Facts for Old and Young Embracing the Natural History and Hygiene of Organic Life*.[5] In addition to a grotesque physical description of what masturbation will cause, Kellogg recommended remedies such as sewing closed the foreskins of older boys and applying "pure carbolic acid to the clitoris" of girls.[6]

Added to this medically inaccurate and destructive perspective is a similarly defective biblical misinterpretation. Some have insisted that masturbation is condemned because of Onan, who "spilled his semen on the ground" (Genesis 38:9). However, it is easy to observe from the context (vv. 6–10) that Onan was not stimulating himself but rather withdrew from his sister-in-law Tamar and ejaculated on the ground. This whole scenario has much to do with Levitical law and nothing to do with God's view of masturbation. There is no biblical reference that specifically addresses the practice by name.

CONTRASTING VIEWPOINTS

Viewpoints about masturbation vary widely in both religious and secular cultures. Consider for example the following sampling from selected books:

SECULAR BOOKS

Sex on Campus: "Short of masturbating so frequently that you rub your skin raw, there are no negative side effects to masturbation. In fact, the opposite seems to be true. Masturbation has been shown to enhance self-worth, release tension, and broaden people's knowledge of their own sexual responses. Sex therapists may even prescribe certain masturbation practices as a way of helping men increase their staying power with a partner and a way for women to learn how to be orgasmic during sex with a partner."[7]

Sex in America: "[There are] those who feel that masturbation must be bad for them or for their children or those who feel that not masturbating is a measure of will power and triumph over a nearly overwhelming drive. On the other side, there are those who feel that masturbation is not a crime or a vice. But even the most liberal tend to see masturbation as an activity that is appropriate only for the young or those without partners."[8]

SPIRITUALLY ORIENTED BOOKS

Christians in the Wake of the Sexual Revolution: "Masturbation can become an obsessive and enslaving habit fueling and refueling the fire of one's lusts and lowering people to sex object status. It can become entangled with the obsessive compulsion of pornography and lead to increasingly perverse functions and desires."[9]

Sex: Desiring the Best: "Masturbation is the selfish and unnatural way of sexual release. Therefore, masturbation has no place in the life of a follower of Jesus Christ."[10]

Sex: It's Worth Waiting For: "Masturbation usually does not relieve sexual tension. In the long run, it causes more tension. You see, the more you masturbate, the more you want to masturbate."[11]

Eros Defiled: "Masturbation is not a good thing, but neither is it a heinous thing."[12]

Sex, Dating, and Love: "Since masturbation centers the sex expression on the self, it is thought to be an abuse of the purpose of sex. It is not that masturbation is evil or bad in itself. It's just that it violates the principle that sex is to be shared."[13]

Handling Your Hormones: "Masturbation is practically universal. It isn't the gross sin some people think it is, yet at times, it can have a negative side to it."[14]

This litany of viewpoints is not designed to cause confusion but to stir one's thoughts about a personal approach to the topic. Ultimately each individual must develop a personal position on the subject.

TOWARD BALANCE AND HEALING

An element that often accompanies masturbation is the presence of visual erotica in the form of photographs or videos. The problem with this lies in the potential for viewing others as objects rather than as people. Another negative associated with erotica is the tendency to compare people in real life with the retouched photos of silicone-injected, cosmetic-surgery-perfected super models. Against such medical feats no one can compete. The search for physical perfection can often lead to frustration, disappointment, and unfulfilled expectations.

In addition to erotica, masturbation is often linked to sexual fantasy. Fantasy involves allowing the mind to create imaginary sexual scenarios involving the fantasizer and a real or imagined individual. To resist a temptation to fantasy, we must construct a personal, practical paradigm to help us make the right decisions. This is especially true for those who are spiritually alive and have a high sense of morality.

Anyone who has helped care for children knows that it is not unusual for children, especially boys, to fondle their private parts during bath time. Such fondling is as natural as an adult's scratching an arm or leg to relieve an itch. When an adult scratches an itch, this does not usually involve sexual fantasy. If masturbation were nothing more than childlike curiosity, there would probably be fewer concerns about its rightness or wrongness. The problems usually emerge when lust becomes involved to the point of devaluing rather than enhancing personhood. It is important to remember that in order to experience and embrace abundant life, one must also embrace personal discipline in all areas. This means, for example, that sexually fantasizing each night about a coworker at your job would not be a healthy activity (Matthew 5:28). However, author Rick Stedman points out the following: "To think of a nondescript person in sexual terms, such as imagining what it would be like to be kissed, to imagine what it feels like to be held . . . may not be sinful."[15] His point is that it is not wrong to dream about something that would not be wrong to act upon.

Another angle to consider is that in all men there is a normal buildup of semen. If this is not released, the body naturally releases it through nocturnal emissions, or "wet dreams." Thus, according to Stedman, masturbation "can be right when used as a limited temporary program of self-control to avoid lust. Masturbation used in moderation without lust for the purpose of retaining one's purity is not immoral."[16] Of course, a "limited temporary program" could possibly turn into a regular addictive practice under certain circumstances.

It is interesting to observe that most of the writers and speakers who wholeheartedly denounce sexual self-stimulation in any form and under any circumstances are usually married. The bottom line is that single people must come to terms with their own understanding of masturbation and provide honest answers to honest questions such as the following:

- Does my masturbation devalue, objectify, or dehumanize someone else?
- Does masturbation control me, or do I control it?
- Does masturbation distance me from meaningful relationships with others?
- Does masturbation in any way bring dishonor to me, my friends, my family, my acquaintances, or my God?

Is it possible to engage in nonlustful masturbation? If I feel guilty about masturbation, is that guilt socially induced or divinely induced?

An honest struggle with these questions and others should lead to some helpful answers for the single who is seeking a clear understanding of the subject. For those who know that masturbation has become a problem, perhaps the following steps will help:

- *Watch what you view.* Select carefully what you choose to see regarding sexually suggestive literature, television, videos, or real people.
- *Mind what you hear.* Popular radio has a strong tendency to paint sexually suggestive scenarios that can make us feel left out if we are not sexually involved with a dating partner.
- *Consider whom you hang out with.* Are your associates exerting a healthy influence on you? If not, find some who do.
- *Seek help beyond yourself.* Confide in a friend of the same gender who can hold you accountable in these matters.
- *Use divine resources.* Victory in any area of struggle is attainable through a personal commitment to God accompanied by regular Scripture reading and prayer.

LET'S TALK!

1. What guidelines does 1 Corinthians 6:12 imply regarding masturbation?
2. Why is the subject of masturbation so seldom discussed?

3. Why do you think there is such a wide variety of opinions and attitudes about masturbation?
4. How do you feel about the use of visually erotic materials?
5. How do you feel about reading erotic novels or romance books?
6. Do you feel that fantasizing about a particular individual is harmful or harmless? Are there any limits?
7. Is there a difference between fantasizing about a known person and fantasizing about an imaginary person?
8. Do you think it is wrong to have lustful feelings and thoughts toward one's fiancé?
9. Is masturbation an option to someone who perhaps will never marry?
10. What do you feel is the most challenging aspect of the masturbation question?

Chapter 8

DATE RAPE

Some Men's Fantasy, Every Woman's Nightmare

Gregg and Marcia had dated for six months before the night they attended a party sponsored by Gregg's fraternity. More people turned out for the party than was expected, so the hotel ballroom was packed. The atmosphere was electric with excitement. The band was smokin'... and so were several of the partygoers, including Marcia. Gregg was usually rather reserved, but on this night he was unusually animated as he matched Marcia's skill on the dance floor. Perhaps Gregg's attitude alteration was due to the four trips he made to sample the "mystery punch."

At about 3:00 A.M., they left the party, and Gregg decided to stop by his apartment to get something to eat before taking Marcia home. After a quick snack of microwaved subs, Marcia decided to relax for a moment. Gregg's plush, oversized sofa felt warm and comfortable after such an exhausting evening. So Marcia reclined and relaxed her sleek, caramel-colored body on the sofa with her arms framing her head. Just as Gregg came back from putting the dishes in the sink, Marcia deeply inhaled, exhaled, and drew up one knee as she glanced invitingly at Gregg. The sight did something to Gregg. As he slid onto the sofa beside her, they exchanged a warm, moist kiss. One thing led to another. Twenty minutes later, something clicked in Marcia, and she said softly, "No, Gregg." Gregg continued his advances while simultaneously kissing Marcia to keep her mouth closed. Just before Gregg entered her, Marcia mumbled something in protest, but nothing clear enough to make Gregg stop. Gregg finished quickly and lay exhausted beside her. After a minute of silence, her only words were, "Take me home."

Was it date rape or not?

What, in fact, is date rape? As the story of Gregg and Marcia illustrates, "date rape" is a form of rape because it takes place against the woman's will. Rightly or wrongly, the fact that it has a distinctive name somehow makes it seem different. Perhaps one difference is that date rape does not often entail the kind of rage and violence that attends other acts of rape. Indeed, to the offender, rape is not at its core an act arising from sexual desire at all but rather arises from distorted emotional needs for power and control. By contrast, date rape usually involves sexual desire.

In America 22% of women report being forced to submit to a sexual act at some time.[1] Only 2% of men report being forced into having sex. Almost one-third of college students report having experienced forced sex.[2] It may or may not come as a surprise that among the women who had a sexual act forced upon them, only 4% of the instances involved a stranger, 9% a spouse, 19% an acquaintance, 22% someone the victim knew well, and 46% someone with whom the victim was in love.[3] Many of the reasons for date rape may be rooted in the myths and misunderstandings surrounding it.

MYTHS AND MISUNDERSTANDINGS

Misunderstandings can be damaging and even deadly. Following are eight myths that can contribute to date rape.

"NO MEANS YES."

A common misunderstanding in cases of date rape occurs when the woman typically says no and the guy thinks she really means yes. He "reasons" that she really wants him, but is only saying no to keep from appearing too easy. Although some women may play this dangerous game, the best bet for the brother is to assume that "no" means NO.

"SEXY CLOTHES MEAN YES."

Some men reason, "She must want me, or she wouldn't have dressed that way." This myth can serve as a warning to women as well as a message to men. Seductive clothing can send unintended messages. However, even if a woman goes on a date wearing a low-cut midriff top with low-rise stretch pants, it should not automatically be assumed that she wants the evening to end in bed with her date.

"A LOOSE REPUTATION MEANS YES."

After a workout at the health club, Lamont and Omar were just chillin' in the locker room catching up on the latest. Lamont casually mentioned how two weeks ago he had taken Laura out for a Sunday afternoon drive and they ended up at sunset on the lakeshore, sitting in the car and sipping wine coolers with a Maxwell groove on the CD. Lamont said that even though it was their first time out together, Laura gave it up there in the back of the Benz. Omar teased Lamont for being "high schoolish," but he nevertheless filed that scenario in the back of his mind. When he went out with the same Laura that next weekend, he was indignant when he made his move and she made her move— in the opposite direction. What he failed to understand was that although Laura was still Laura, Omar was certainly not Lamont. And even if he were Lamont, she still maintained the right to say no. This leads us to our next myth.

"PREVIOUS SEX MEANS FUTURE SEX."

An old saying in some male circles goes like this: "If you've been there once, you can always go back." The truth is that in some cases, the fact that you have been there once may be the very reason that you're not allowed back again. Assumptions can be disastrous when it comes to sex. There are many diehard players out there who have compiled an extensive repertoire of tricks in the art of seduction. Since these tactics have worked every time in the past, it is assumed that no one could resist them for long. A woman who initially resists a man's advances becomes even more attractive and desirable because she offers more of a challenge.

"STRONG WILLS MEAN YES."

Unfortunately, it has not occurred to some people that the other person's opinion must be considered before engaging in sex. Beware of the person who frequently and sometimes violently insists on doing things his or her way. The "relationship forecast" regarding this person might read as "thunderstorms likely, cloudy and cold with a 90% chance of rain."

"BIG BILLS MEAN YES."

Some men believe that anybody can be bought if there is enough flash of the cash. It is true that some women seem to have a severe case of money on the brain, but even in such instances, it is culturally, morally, and spiritually unethical to presume that liberally sharing one's financial or material assets permits automatic access to another person's physical or sexual assets.

"BIG BUILDS MEAN YES."

Marvin Macho was third runner-up for *Mr. Muscle Magazine*'s regional talent search two years ago. Since then, he has just assumed that any woman who is privileged to be seen in his company outside the confines of the workout room must desperately be after his body just like those Mr. Muscle talent scouts. I say, "Come on, Marvin. Now that you are buffed up, grow up."

"BIG THRILLS MEAN YES."

Have you ever heard the one that goes like this: "Baby, we've gone too far for us to stop this thing right now." This perspective plays on the sympathy of the woman by requesting her to help relieve him of the "agonizing" sexual pressure that she just helped to create. This, however, is also an illegitimate excuse. There is always the invigorating option of a cold shower or four laps around the block.

CAUSES

What would cause someone to rape one's date? Although the answers to this question can be as varied as human personality, there are some patterns. The reasons for date rape may fall into one single category listed below or may encompass a variety of reasons.

POWER AND CONTROL

Many people who rape their dates are hungry for power and control. Rather than being content with simply relating to the woman, the line is crossed and manipulation occurs. Usually there are subtle signs that identify a person with a controlling personality. The guy may repeatedly ignore his partner's suggestions or belittle her opinions. The power-hungry controller has a perpetual need to be right and expresses an extremely negative reaction when confronted or corrected.

INSECURITY

A character trait that tends to go along with power and control is insecurity. Acts of control are sometimes expressed to cover or compensate for a lack of a sense of security or self-confidence. People with this trait are sometimes drawn to weaker, more vulnerable persons who seem to be easily dominated.

REVENGE

Most abusers have themselves been abused in some way in the past. If a man has been physically abused as a child or has been emotionally jilted by a woman as an adult, he could be driven to the point of seeking subconscious revenge or reenactment through committing rape.

ENVIRONMENT

Sometimes men become conditioned by their environment to the point of believing that "if she doesn't give it up, you've got to take it." When this kind of thinking is presented and accepted as the norm, the man consequently does not feel that his actions are extreme. Locker-room bragging sessions can also produce the unhealthy idea that forced sex yields a greater thrill than consensual sex. Regardless of the reasons behind date rape, such behavior is absolutely unjustifiable.

HEALING

Deep wounds may be difficult to heal, and the journey toward recovery may be difficult, but both are still possible. Some rape victims have discovered empowerment through helping other rape victims to achieve emotional and psychological recovery. Date rape can cause extensive emotional pain and psychological damage, but there is hope and help for healing.

COUNSELING AND SUPPORT

It is important not to endure the pain of rape alone. Sharing feelings with a competent and caring counselor can ease the load and redirect one's energies toward recovery. Group counseling can involve others who have experienced rape and can understand and empathize.

HOT LINES

If person-to-person counseling is not an available or attractive option, perhaps telephone counseling would help meet the need. Below are two organizations that specialize in rape counseling:

The Rape Crisis Center 24-hour Hot Link (210) 349–72735
National Rape Crisis Hot Line (800) 656–4673

GUILT

It is common for a victim of rape to blame herself for what happened. This ultimate invasion of privacy produces a sense of shame and guilt. An unhealthy dose of false guilt can express itself in self-doubt: "Maybe this would not have happened if I had not worn that dress, gone to that place, or said that thing." The conclusion of many such internal interrogations is often, "It must have been my fault." While every woman should use wisdom and caution in a relationship, there is still no excuse for rape, and the victim is *not* the one to blame.

RESPONSE

Every woman must decide for herself what recourse is right in the aftermath of a rape. Should charges be pressed? (If so, physical evidence is important.) Am I safe from future encounters? How will I respond the next time we meet? Who else needs to be told about this? Date rape is a multifaceted issue with an unlimited number of angles that should be explored.

FORGIVENESS

Forgiveness may initially seem like a most unlikely element in response to rape. However, forgiveness is not for the benefit of the abuser, but for the benefit of the victim. Forgiveness is a spiritual and psychological force that releases the injured party to pursue total healing. The longer we hold on to the hurts, the longer it takes to heal our hurts.

Time is the great eraser of the circumstantial graffiti we acquire on this wall called life. Although there may always be traces of pain in our memory, the longer we live and give, the stronger we will grow.

PREVENTION

Although it is impossible to ultimately control another person's actions, caution and wisdom are always in order. One of the most prevalent factors in date rape is the presence of alcohol. Alcohol often provides the impetus to just "let sex happen." As noted earlier, one survey reported that 47% of college students had participated in sex when they had not planned to, but did so as a result of alcohol. The Center on Addiction and Substance Abuse at Columbia University reports that "in 90 percent of campus rapes, the assailant, the victim, or both had been drinking."[4]

Along with mutual alcohol abstinence, another preventative could be to thoroughly research your date. Before going on the date, ask some pertinent questions. If possible, talk to his friends and maybe even a former date. Some other tips are to begin and end your date at a public location other than your place or his place. Daytime dates are usually safer than nighttime ones, especially early in the relationship. Taking precautions is not a sign of paranoia, but an indication of maturity.

LET'S TALK!

1. What are some of the reasons behind date rape?
2. Discuss the scenario with Gregg and Marcia at the beginning of the chapter. Was anyone at fault? If so, who? Was it rape? Could it have been avoided?
3. Which of the myths and misunderstandings about date rape are the most prevalent among singles?
4. Should a woman have the right to wear any kind of clothes she desires? Does the same hold true for a man?

5. Do you think that all date rapes should be reported to the police? If not, what should be done?
6. What could you do to assist a friend who has experienced date rape?
7. How would you deal with a friend or acquaintance who has committed date rape?
8. What implications does Romans 8:37–39 have for a victim of date rape?

Chapter 9

HOMOSEXUALITY

A Challenge for Gays and Straights

Entire books have been written on the highly controversial subject of homosexuality. Since homosexuality is not our central focus, we will simply provide a brief glimpse of a few of the more crucial aspects of this topic. One would think that a good place to begin understanding homosexuality is at the point of definition. However, even trying to formulate a conclusive definition proves to be a challenge. The difficulty lies in the question of whether the term *homosexual* should describe someone's inner desires, outer behavior, self-identity, or a combination of these traits.[1]

The word *homosexual* comes from a Greek term that means "the same."[2] For the sake of brevity, when we use the word *homosexual* or *gay* here, it will refer generically to a male or female who actively and physically participates in a sexual relationship with a person of the same gender. At times we will use the word *lesbian* to designate a female.

The items below reflect the wide range of speculation about the possible factors that produce homosexuality:

- Biological inheritance
- Social inheritance
- Initial "shaping" experience[3]
- Clinging or domineering mother
- Distant or abusive father
- Rape or incest

- Social rejection by peers of the same gender
- Social acceptance by the gay community
- Innate tendency to prefer the same gender

This list could be much longer, but the truth is that there has not been enough conclusive research on this subject to be definitive in psychological or biological terms. Until this is achieved, we must go with what we do know and with what we can see. That absence of certainty adds to the emotional climate in which discussion of the topic usually takes place. A lack of knowledge is the breeding ground of fear, and fear tends to distort reason. In addition, if one is insecure in one's own sexuality, it is easy to be nervous about someone else's. Let us consider a few assumptions that have given rise to some of the myths about homosexuality.

MYTHS AND MISCONCEPTIONS

MYTH #1: YOU CAN ALWAYS IDENTIFY A HOMOSEXUAL BY THE WAY HE OR SHE LOOKS, ACTS, OR TALKS.

The media have generally portrayed gay males using a wimpy, lisping, bent-wrist stereotype. Although some gay males may fit this description, other acknowledged homosexuals are just the opposite and outwardly appear to be quite macho. Moreover, not every person who exhibits these characteristics is homosexual.

MYTH #2: HOMOSEXUALS ARE USUALLY THE CHILD MOLESTERS.

A homosexual's love interest, like a heterosexual's, is usually directed toward peers of roughly the same age rather than children. Also, whereas child molesters are usually impelled by a tendency toward power, control, and violence, gay men and lesbians are generally more prone to peacefulness.

MYTH #3: HOMOSEXUALS CANNOT CONTROL THEIR ACTIONS.

Because of discipline, we typically do not act on everything we feel. If we did, a great deal more of us might find ourselves in prison. Can you imagine the chaos if everyone acted on every impulse? Sometimes behavior and habits are rationalized by saying, "I was born this way." Some overeaters may say they cannot refuse food, or some unmarried heterosexuals may say they cannot refuse sexual temptation. Yet, as long as we have the will for it, we can usually regulate our actions no matter how strong the impulse. From a spiritual perspective, regardless of the way we may have been born, there is still a need to be spiritually born again.

MYTH #4: ONCE GAY, ALWAYS GAY.

Most current research clearly reveals that some people have a tendency to move from being exclusively heterosexual to bisexual to homosexual and sometimes all the way back around. If it were impossible to alter one's sexual preference, that sociological scenario would be impossible.

MYTH #5: GAY MEN HATE WOMEN, AND LESBIANS HATE MEN.

Most gays and lesbians indiscriminately relate to others on a social and professional level without regard to social preference. With homosexuals as well as heterosexuals, anger, and thus the hate, usually surfaces with those who have been emotionally or sexually abused and therefore associate this tragic experience with a particular gender.[4]

THREE VIEWPOINTS

Whether or not the aforementioned myths are consciously present in our thinking, most people reflect one of the following responses to the subject of homosexuality:

1. BAN IT!

People with a "ban it" mentality tend to feel that homosexuals have no right to exist and should therefore be forever banned from the face of the earth. These people would like to close their eyes and have it all go away so that there would be no need to deal with gays or lesbians in public life. Obviously, this view is quite unrealistic in that homosexuality is not likely ever to disappear.

2. FAN IT!

People who have a "fan it" mentality tend not only to favor homosexuality as a desirable lifestyle, but also to flaunt it and compel other gays to "come out of the closet"—that is, to declare their homosexuality publicly. These activists are on a mission to march, make waves, disturb the peace, change rules, and in general do whatever it takes to gain public acceptance of homosexuals. Ironically, some of those who want to fan it are driven to this point by those who want to ban it. Persecution can prompt retaliation. Sometimes this retaliation occurs when homosexuals accuse all who disagree with homosexuality of being *homophobic*—literally, "afraid of homosexuality." Although homophobia is a real and pervasive phenomenon, one should not be automatically labeled as homophobic simply because one does not condone a homosexual lifestyle.

3. UNDERSTAND IT!

Proverbs 4:7 tells us, "Get wisdom. Though it cost all you have, get understanding." Many of life's problems and struggles could be simplified if we would make the effort required to see beneath the surface of the issues involved. Some homosexuals suffer the painful double jeopardy of not understanding themselves in addition to not being understood by the wider community. John White states that "the deepest longing in the heart of a homosexual is the longing to be known, to be loved, and to be accepted."[5] These are very similar to the longings of heterosexuals; the problem arises when homosexuals seek to fulfill them in a way that violates God's perfect will. Like heterosexual premarital sex, homosexual sex is still sex out of context.

The beautiful thing is that we can understand a person even though we may not approve of a person's tendencies or characteristics.

AVENUES TOWARD UNDERSTANDING

The following represents my deductions and discoveries as a result of an honest effort to more clearly understand homosexuality:

THERE ARE MANY DIFFERENT EXPRESSIONS OF THE HOMOSEXUAL EXPERIENCE.

It is a mistake to lump all homosexual experiences into a single category. For example:

- Some have experienced homosexual desires or fantasies or have become sexually aroused at the sight, thought, or touch of a person of the same gender.
- Some have had an experience in childhood that involved homosexuality—perhaps sexual abuse by an adult or incest or experimentation with another child.
- Some have temporarily resorted to homosexual activities as a result of limited contact with the other gender, through incarceration or noncoeducational schools or some armed services.

It is helpful for heterosexuals to recognize at least three categories of homosexuals. According to Santoria Alsup, there are "militants," "moderates," and "strugglers."[6] Militants are those who forcefully make their presence known and diligently work to obtain legal affirmation of their lifestyle. These are the ones who march in Gay Pride parades. The moderates' stance is, "You don't bother me and I won't bother you." They just want to be left alone and not hindered from exercising freedom of lifestyle. Strugglers are those who often feel that they do not fit comfortably into either the heterosexual or the homosexual community. They may desire to live as a heterosexual but feel such a strong pull in another direction that it sometimes seems like a tug-of-war. The person who fits into this category is probably, among the three, the one most open to personal and spiritual growth and change.

HOMOSEXUAL ROLES AND PHYSICAL ACTS ARE OFTEN UNCONSCIOUS IMITATIONS OF HETEROSEXUAL ROLES AND PHYSICAL ACTS.

Without becoming unnecessarily graphic, it is interesting to note that gay and lesbian partners often adopt traditional masculine and feminine roles as they relate to each other. This is observable in their "soft/passive" versus "tough/aggressive" physical appearance and behavior patterns. Gay males who engage in anal sex often adopt and prefer one position over the other: male (giver) or female (receiver). No matter how hard one may try to deny it, there is simply no way to avoid the fact that men were specifically crafted to fit and complement women sexually and relationally. Women, likewise, were specifically crafted to fit and complement men sexually and relationally. Any expression apart from this is at best a mere imitation of the real thing.

THERE ARE SUBTLE DIFFERENCES BETWEEN LESBIAN WOMEN AND GAY MEN.

As is the nature of heterosexuals, gay men tend to be driven by physical attractions whereas lesbians tend to long for emotional ties. Not surprisingly, there is a tendency for gay male relationships to last a shorter length of time and to break up more often. John White writes, "If inconstancy and infidelity plague the straight world, they plague the gay world to a far greater degree."[7] In one national collegiate survey, female heterosexuals reported an average of 5.5 sex partners during a lifetime, while male heterosexuals reported a 6.5 average. But female gays/bisexuals reported an average of 8.0 sexual partners and male gays/bisexuals reported an average of 14.4 sexual partners during their lifetimes. Twelve percent of all the heterosexuals reported having had at least twenty-five sexual partners, compared with more than 22% of all the gays/bisexuals in the survey.[8]

IT IS UNWISE TO VIEW ONE'S LIFE FROM PRIMARILY A SEXUAL PERSPECTIVE.

Regardless of our sexual orientation, it is a mistake to base our entire identity or lifestyle on any brand or form of sexuality. *No* aspect of sex is important enough or comprehensive enough to define our total personhood.

Betty Berzon, a counselor and author who is also a lesbian, warns about gay couples falling into the "body-type trap": "I have heard many rationales for sex outside the relationship. Often it is about the hunt, which is usually a hunt for personal validation." Berzon describes this trap as occurring when one becomes fixated on an idealized body image stemming from photography or personal fantasies. Consequently every prospective partner is judged according to this image. She makes the point that an overemphasis on sexuality can cause lesbians to become depressed and drug dependent. This overemphasis can cause gay men to be left with a string of flings while still searching for a new and more physically attractive partner.[9]

HOMOSEXUALS WHO ARE STRUGGLING NEED LESS NAME-CALLING AND MORE HEALTHY AND CONSTRUCTIVE RELATIONSHIPS WITH STRAIGHT PEOPLE OF THEIR OWN GENDER.

Perhaps you have at some point repeated the comical line about God's making "Adam and Eve, not Adam and Steve." Although this line may seem humorous to heterosexuals, it can be very painful to struggling homosexuals. If a gay person wanted help in dealing with sexual tendencies, do you think he or she would be inclined to confide in a person who would repeat such insensitive words?

TOWARD HEALING

Struggling gay men and women who desire to change can take some very basic steps toward personal growth and healing.

- Conduct a personal "inner view," in which you look inside yourself and your personal history as far as you can remember, in order to better understand yourself and your desires. (A competent and compassionate counselor might also be helpful in this process.)
- Admit or recognize your struggle. Obstacles can be more quickly overcome when we identify and acknowledge them.
- In the rare instances of hermaphroditism (possessing the genitals of both sexes), the most reasonable and least confusing approach would be to simply make a choice of one gender and stick with it.
- Make a personal decision to make a change. Nothing will be altered until there is a personal decision for change.
- Close the door to past relationships and burn old bridges of temptation. Habits are often rekindled through associating with former friends. Make a clean sweep of your relationships and remove their debris from your life.
- Drop old labels and verbally speak positive power and hope into your life. Use your mind and your mouth to declare your new identity.
- Tap into God's power to assist you in your journey as the struggle continues. You may never be completely free from temptation;

few people ever accomplish this feat. But through God's help, a victorious life is possible, one day at a time.

LET'S TALK!

1. Why is the subject of homosexuality so controversial?
2. Which of the five listed myths about homosexuality have you heard most frequently? Do you feel that any of these myths are actually true?
3. Do you disagree with any of the myths? Are there others you would like to add?
4. Do you see any advantages in the development of platonic (nonsexual) friendships between heterosexuals and homosexuals? Would you consider such a friendship?
5. What are some characteristics of homophobia? How can homophobia be overcome?
6. Do you believe that homosexuals can change their behavior? If so, should they change?
7. If you are a homosexual, what do you agree with in this chapter? What statements do you feel are biased or inaccurate?
8. Some homosexuals say that Jesus is silent on the subject of homosexuality. What do you think?
9. Do the things that Jesus said about fornication also apply to homosexual behaviors?
10. Romans 1:24–28 directly addresses the subject of homosexuality. After reading it, discuss the spiritual principles you observe.

Chapter 10

BREAKING UP WITHOUT BREAKING DOWN
Halting Unhealthy Relationships—
No [Straight]jacket Required

Have you ever been in a relationship that broke up before it grew up? Perhaps you are now in a relationship that is in dire need of emergency CPR. Why is it that so many relationships fail? In her insightful book *Too Good to Leave, Too Bad to Stay*, Mira Kirshenbaum explains it this way:

> In the beginning you meet someone and fall in love. As you fly through the air, falling head over heels, you're thinking to yourself, she's wonderful, she's special, she's great. The rocket of love is hard to launch without this fuel of mutual admiration. But what goes up must come down. Just as there's always a difference between campaign promises and the real deal, once he's in office, once you've elected yourself an official couple, you arrive at that promised land of intimacy you have been seeking so avidly. But time turns intimacy into familiarity, and we all know what familiarity breeds.[1]

Effective and satisfying male-female relationships require extensive work. But they sometimes reach a breaking point when one or both parties decide that the work outweighs the worth. A wide variety of factors can create such a condition, but here we will focus on only a few of the basic and most frequent causes.

FACTORS THAT CAN CONTRIBUTE TO A BREAKUP

SELFISHNESS

Selfishness is a broad term that actually encompasses many of the factors mentioned below. When a person displays a pattern of selfishness, it is like the slow but steady drip of a poisonous "IV" into the partner's veins of self-esteem. Extensive damage can occur before the victim realizes the danger and disconnects from the relationship. The only other option is to maintain this fatal attraction and evolve into yet another relationship zombie. The various aspects of selfishness will be addressed more extensively in the next chapter.

RELATIONSHIP DRIFTING

Renee was initially attracted to Ty because he was a professional football player. She loved the choice seating at games, she loved chatting with the other players' wives and girlfriends, and most of all, she loved the feeling of "star status" she experienced whenever she accompanied Ty to a team-sponsored social event. After two years of togetherness, Renee quit her job as a secretary, enrolled in school, and pursued her dream of a legal career. During the very first semester, Renee began to notice increasing distance between the two of them. She and Ty spent less and less time together as the relationship ditch between them widened into a valley of separation. They finally broke up. Renee still believed that Ty was a very nice guy, but it was clear that her priorities had shifted to a degree that he became less complementary to her interests and lifestyle.

This couple's differences centered around vocation and education. But relationship drift can be caused by many other factors, from the sexual to the spiritual.

ANOTHER LOVER

One of the most painful relationship breakers is the emergence of another lover. Dating multiple partners may be acceptable if both partners are agreeable to it. However, when one partner violates an expectation of exclusivity, there is a problem. Why do many people seem to dabble in third-party affairs? One possible reason is that outside of marriage, few people talk seriously about expectations of a monogamous relationship. Perhaps there would be fewer problems if the subject of multiple dating were openly and thoroughly discussed. It would not hurt to even write down these expectations and review them periodically. This may sound a bit too serious for the dating level, but what could be more important than keeping our emotional equilibrium when so much time and energy are typically invested in relationships? Dishonesty in relationships undermines trust, and this can lead to the premature and unnecessary death of a relationship.

LACK OF PROGRESS

I remember receiving a "pink slip" once when the woman I was dating determined that our relationship was not progressing quickly enough. Although we had dated for several months and had enjoyed each other's company, there was no ring, no sex, and no promises. She reasoned that since she already had a child from a previous relationship, what she needed was a husband for herself and a father for her son. At the time, that was not something I was willing or ready to provide. Therefore we had an amicable parting of ways with no hard feelings on either side. Nothing was wrong with either of us—we were just not right for each other at that particular time in our lives.

THE PAIN OUTWEIGHS THE PEACE

If you weighed your relationship on a scale that balanced pain and problems on one side, with peace and progress on the other, which side would weigh more? Most people can tolerate only a limited amount of continual pain in a relationship. Although some pain is inevitable and even useful, a healthy relationship should reflect more peace than pain.

ABUSE

One obvious reason for leaving a relationship is abuse—physical, sexual, or emotional. There is no need to tolerate such treatment. Since most abusers have been abused themselves, it is easy to understand how "hurt people can hurt people." People who are dealing with the emotional consequences of abuse suffered in childhood need professional therapy; in the meantime, the partner should not continue to play the role of "victim." Despite promises that "It will never happen again," no relationship is worth the risk of death, injury, or mental breakdown. When evaluating ambivalent relationships, Kirshenbaum advises against putting the relationship on trial as a lawyer would do. Instead, she demonstrates the value of making an informed diagnosis—the way a doctor would do.[2] When a relationship is objectively diagnosed rather than subjectively put on trial, this approach greatly helps to eliminate much of the emotion, denial, accusation, and defensiveness that tends to surround decisions about whether to leave or stay. Below are several other factors that could cloud or complicate a decision.

FACTORS THAT MAKE IT DIFFICULT TO BREAK UP

INSECURITY OR LAZINESS

Some people dread the termination of a relationship because they cannot bear the thought of being emotionally alone. Some may have also become overly comfortable in the relationship and are unwilling to face the prospect of rejoining the "hunt." Insecurity and laziness are not good reasons for remaining in a relationship. Mature relationships are not codependent relationships.

O.P.P.

Decisions to stay or leave can be infinitely complicated by O.P.P.— other people's pressure. Although objective perspectives and advice from others can be helpful, you are the one who must ultimately decide. If other people offer advice, it is okay to consider it and express appreciation for their concern. Beyond that, you should make clear on whose shoulders the decision ultimately rests: yours and your partner's. Needless to say, pressure from your family can be particularly difficult to handle.

SEXUAL TIES

A thrilling sex life can cause a person to invent reasons to stay even when leaving would be a much better choice. Because sex was designed with permanency in mind, sexual ties are not easily broken. Some partners realize this and take advantage of their ability to press all the right buttons and flip all the right switches. If you have been in a sexual relationship that is not consecrated by marriage vows, breaking up is really hard even if you realize that it is the right thing to do both morally and emotionally. There are some actions that can help you in the struggle: Make a definite decision to end the relationship; spend time and distance away from your partner; and seek divine assistance through prayer, fasting, reading, and meditation.

CHILDREN

If a child is involved in the relationship, it is more difficult to make a complete break with a partner. It is important for every child to have healthy contact with both parents where possible and feasible. Both parties should strive to foster good mental health and good emotional development in the children. Parents should seek to be cordial and cooperative if only for the positive advancement of the child.

WHEN YOU INITIATE THE BREAKUP

When you are the person who decides to end the relationship, things can be a bit more predictable and planned. Here are some suggestions to help make the break as painless as possible.

Don't make a rash decision. If you are upset, try to calm down and rationally think and pray through your decision.

Make the break in person. If possible, avoid "Dear John/Dear Jane" letters. Try to put yourself in your partner's place and realize that it is uncaring to be unceremoniously dumped via e-mail. Muster the courage to confront your partner personally.

Be firm but not rude. You need not apologize for your decision; but there is also no need to be nasty. Remember that a controlled person is a powerful person.

State clearly your reasons for leaving. If you don't explain why, the natural next step would be for your partner to arrange another time to ask that question. He or she will want to know your reasons.

Learn from your experience. Never allow your living or your dating to be in vain. Even negative dating experiences can yield valuable lessons.

WHEN YOUR PARTNER INITIATES THE BREAKUP

When someone breaks up with you, the only control you have is your reaction to this move. In such situations a positive attitude is extremely important in order to survive.

Try not to go to pieces. Do not self-destruct emotionally, but you have full permission to have an all-out bawl when you get by yourself. Just let it out. You will feel better and heal quicker.

Keep your esteem intact. Realize that it is the relationship that is over, not your life. Just because you did not fit into the equation of this relationship does not mean you are a failure.

Remove the reminders. If your breakup is a traumatic one and involves deep emotion, it may be good to remove articles or photographs that will continually remind you of what used to be. If you are up to it, place the articles in a shoebox and conduct a ceremonial burial or burning—New Orleans style. Invite some friends along, sing a few victory songs, and lay that old relationship to rest. Afterward you are entitled to celebrate in any positive and constructive way that makes you happy.

Give yourself time. Just as your "ex" did not get inside your emotional system overnight, do not expect him or her to vanish overnight. Take your time, and don't expect life to return completely to "normal" right away.

Don't close up shop. Many who are devastated by recent breakups make the mistake of closing access to all other relationships and social outlets. Although it is unwise to go immediately into another romantic relationship, the sooner you return to normal activities, the quicker you will heal.

Learn from the experience. Take an emotional inventory and write down what you have learned from the experience. What would you do differently? What would you do the same? How can you help someone else who is facing a similar decision? With God's help, you can turn every negative into a positive.

Although breakups are seldom pretty or easy, they should not have to leave us with permanent emotional scars. With a little time and effort, the delicate decision of whether to stay with someone or to leave can be handled with clarity and care.

LET'S TALK!

1. Share an account of a breakup (if it is not overly personal or painful). How did it occur? Was it a healthy or unhealthy breakup?
2. In the scenario of Renee and Ty, what could they have done to salvage their relationship?
3. Describe a type of relationship that would be too good to leave and too bad to stay.
4. What are some keys to deliverance from the shackles of sexual ties?
5. Is it wise to remain casual friends following a breakup? Explain.
6. What are some surefire indicators that it is time for a couple to part ways?
7. How can the pain of a breakup be kept to a minimum or even turned into gain?
8. What implications does Romans 12:17–21 raise with regard to relationship breakups?

Chapter 11

HOW TO RECOGNIZE MR. OR MS. RIGHT

The Plan for Your Man and the Wife for Your Life

The decision to marry is the most crucial social decision one will ever make. It is a very serious decision that will impact virtually every single aspect of one's life. The preparation and perspective we bring to this decision can spell either heaven or hell.

Most schools, churches, and community centers offer a vast array of courses on subjects ranging from computer technology to ancient Egyptian burial customs. But why is there seldom if ever a course on knowing how to recognize and marry the right person? There is a need for practical information on choosing a lifetime mate. The typical marriage stems from a curious combination of coincidence, hormones, peer pressure, economics, age, and tradition. Is it any wonder that approximately half of the marriages in the United States eventually end in divorce? Contemporary customs have made marriage much easier to enter and to exit than they once were. Perhaps one way to lower the divorce rate would be to make it more difficult to begin and to end a marriage. A number of cities, such as Modesto, California, have seen divorce rates fall because of a bold and radical new movement. In these places, clergy and city officials have worked together to jointly adopt a Community Marriage Policy that requires any couples desiring a church wedding to agree to certain stipulations:

- A preparation period of at least four months prior to a wedding
- Biblical instruction on the responsibilities of marriage partners

- Development of a budget and repayment plan for any debts
- Personality temperament analysis tests for the couple
- Counseling with a minister and a mentor couple
- Abstinence from sexual relations during courtship[1]

This voluntary concept of covenant marriage is already officially sanctioned as an option by the state of Louisiana and is being considered by other states. Indeed, marriage works better as a covenant than as a contract. A contract operates from a premise of distrust, whereas a covenant operates from a premise of trust.

It is important never to rush into marriage, and this movement recognizes the need to take time to prepare for it. In his book *Should I Get Married?* M. Blaine Smith identifies some of the important issues affecting marriage readiness:

Values
Family history
Track records
The age question
Independent living experience
Time and money management
Length of acquaintance
Reaction to difficulty
Freedom from addictions
Degree of desperateness[2]

These and other issues deserve a closer look. Choosing a lifetime mate can be an unnerving experience. Like a walk through a minefield, the path toward matrimony may be strewn with a variety of hidden dangers. Smith identifies some of these traps as marriage idealization, unrealistic expectations, and overspiritualization.[3]

Although no marriage partner can be expected to be absolutely perfect, every person contemplating marriage should have a familiar list of "negotiables" and "nonnegotiables" regarding a potential mate. While some traits may be "desirable" in a person, others should be considered mandatory. Many marriages falter because one or more of the unwritten, unspoken "nonnegotiables" was compromised. Write down *exactly* what you *must* have in a mate. Enlarge it, frame it, hang it over your bed if you must. Get in serious touch with the most intimate you and discover what you need in order for your love to survive and to thrive. Whatever you do, don't confuse "relationship necessities" with "relationship accessories."

In her best-selling book *Are You the One for Me?* Barbara De Angelis lists what she calls the six biggest mistakes that are made in the beginning of relationships:

1. We don't ask enough questions.
2. We ignore warning signs and potential problems.
3. We make premature compromises.
4. We give in to lust blindness.
5. We give in to material seduction.
6. We put commitment before compatibility.[4]

Perhaps one or more of these relationship mistakes is familiar to you. Several of them have already been addressed in this book. All too often in dating relationships as well as in marriage, we exert great energy, concern, and effort to repair a relationship while failing to regularly maintain the health of a relationship and avoid preventable problems. The relationships with the best chances for success are the relationships in which both parties are already relatively mature. The type of mate preferred at age nineteen is usually not the same type preferred at age twenty-nine. The obvious reason for this is because of the growth and change that takes place in all of us.

In Prophetess Juanita Bynahm's "No More Sheets" message delivered at a T. D. Jakes Singles Conference, she explained that God revealed to her that she was not yet ready for marriage. The reason: She was not single yet. Though you may be unmarried, God desires a spiritual unconditional commitment to him before matching you with one of his sons or daughters.[5]

When I was single, I was always curious about how married couples knew that they were right for each other. Upon asking them this question, by far the most frequent response contained those three classic words: "You'll just know." This response was very frustrating to me because it left me with no new insight or information. I resolved that if I ever got married, I would develop some practical guidelines for deciding on a lifetime marriage partner. The twelve steps below reflect my findings in the process of my engagement and marriage to my wonderful wife, Coreen.

TWELVE STEPS TO RECOGNIZING GOD'S WIFE FOR YOUR LIFE AND GOD'S PLAN FOR YOUR MAN

1. THE TEST OF THE WORD (PSALM 119:105)

Many of the answers we seek about relationship choices have already been provided in the Bible. Has the Word been carefully and prayerfully searched with the faith and expectation that God will reveal and confirm his will?

What a relief to know that the gift of life did not arrive without written instructions. The Bible contains a considerable amount of insight regarding wise choices for marriage. A few examples follow.

WISE CHOICES

A. A well-chosen mate is one who pleases God (Ecclesiastes 2:26).
B. A well-chosen mate is one who can experience anger without being controlled by it and does not allow harsh feelings to continue for days (Ephesians 4:26).
C. A well-chosen mate is one who has a job! Love is a wonderful thing, but love alone will not buy groceries. A lazy mate is a burden, but an industrious mate is a blessing (Proverbs 13:4; 2 Thessalonians 3:10).

UNWISE CHOICES

A. An ill-chosen mate is one who is sexually promiscuous. Marriage alone will not automatically reform a loose person's ways. Although behavior change is possible, it must be adequately demonstrated prior to the marriage (Proverbs 6:25–35).
B. An ill-chosen mate is one who has an argumentative and complaining spirit. A person who always has something negative to say will be a pain to live with for the rest of one's life (Proverbs 21:9; 27:15–17).

C. An ill-chosen mate is one who is not compassionate and does not strive to truly understand one's partner. Mutual understanding is mandatory for an effective marriage (1 Peter 3:7–9).

Jo Lynn Pool's sentiments summarize the wisdom of trusting God's divine directions in the choice of a mate. She says that a good man (or woman) is hard to find—unless we ask God to be the head of our search committee.[6]

2. THE TEST OF PRAYER (MATTHEW 7:7)

Have I immersed myself in a serious labor of prayer in order to understand God's direction?

Like an airplane with a broken radio or a defective radar system, it is very dangerous for a single person to risk the rigors of marriage without the benefit of constant contact with life's ultimate control tower. In this decade of hectic schedules and dizzying deadlines, it is sometimes only in the reflective and introspective moments of prayer that we can experience solitude and the honest, truthful realism that emerges when we are surrounded by silence.

God desires to provide us with answers to life's questions even more than we desire to receive those answers. But for us to hear from God, we must first be in the right position. That position is one of submission. In old Western movies, when the authorities finally corner the evasive outlaw, the sheriff shouts a statement like this: "You are surrounded! Throw down your gun and come out with your hands up!" We must realize that all our lives we have been surrounded by God's love and, although we have broken God's laws, it is not God's desire to kill us but to heal us and bring us back alive. Yet, before that can happen, we must throw aside our worldly weapons of selfishness and pride so that we can come out with hands raised high in sweet surrender to the compelling authority of God's love.

3. THE TEST OF PEACE (PHILIPPIANS 4:6 - 7)

Is there a serene flow of peace, trust, and contentment about the relationship and its surrounding circumstances?

I am convinced that within each person is a built-in "early warning system" for relationships. The purpose of this system is to alert us to any potential dangers lurking within the scope of our decision-making process. If we consistently heed the promptings of this system, it becomes even more sensitive and accurate. But if we ignore our inner warnings, the system becomes weaker, less accurate, and eventually mute.

Another analogy that may communicate this idea more clearly involves the traffic light. When considering a lifetime commitment, we may sense a "red light," a "green light," or a "yellow light." The key is to obey each of these signals and stop, go, or slow down. When relationship drivers obey the signals, the relationship traffic flows smoothly. But when someone decides to drive against a red light, to stop on a green light, or to hurry through a yellow light, relationship accidents inevitably occur. Remember, our inner signals are there to help us, not to harm us.

4. THE TEST OF COMMUNICATION *(JAMES 1:19 - 20)*

Is it easy to discuss both tough and tender topics and to address problems together through open discussion in a grudge-free atmosphere?

Every relationship eventually encounters those "hot potato" topics that instantly raise the blood pressure. The question is not *whether* a relationship will ever encounter these threats to good communication, but how they will be handled when they arise. Having too many subjects in a closed closet can produce distance and isolation between partners. Good communication is crucial to a healthy relationship. Stifled communication hinders growth. The free and open sharing of ideas, feelings, fears, and desires between a couple is like a fireplace inside a house. If anything blocks the chimney, there will be problems inside. To keep a marriage "smoke free," let the communication flow freely.

5. THE TEST OF COMPLEMENTARY VALUE *(1 CORINTHIANS 12:14 - 23)*

Are we compatible with each other? Do we regard each other with a sense of value and worth?

This test is actually a combination of two related matters: compatibility and worth. Compatibility refers to the ability of a couple to function and flow in a manner that is mutually beneficial. Like a duet involving two musical instruments, compatible couples complement each other without crowding each other or competing with each other.

Imagine your relationship as a two-sided balancing scale. Compatibility involves a healthy balance between similarity and difference. On one side of this relationship scale there must be an ample number of basic things held in common in order to stir interest and avoid clashes. This is particularly important in terms of a person's basic background and values as illustrated by the following:

- Similar philosophy of life in general
- Similar basic goals and priorities in life
- Similar moral and spiritual values
- Similar family background or expectation
- Similar financial background or expectation

Couples who are not radically different from each other in the basics of life tend to be more successful in the long run.

On the other side of the relationship scale there is the issue of difference. It has been said that if the two people in a relationship are exactly the same, one is unnecessary. Herein lies the beauty and the benefit of difference: A powerful couple is one in which the strengths and abilities of one person compensate for the weaknesses and shortcomings of the other. An example is the pairing of a talkative, outgoing woman with a strong, quiet, laid-back man. It could mean a man with great ideas but few planning skills matched with a woman who may not be as imaginative but is excellent in organization and following through. These are examples of differences working *for* the couple rather than against them. Over time, a sense of complementarity in a marriage enables growth in the areas where the partner is strong, and one's weaknesses tend to diminish. Marriage should be a duet, not a duel.

The other aspect of the complementary value concept is worth. Although it may be primarily unspoken, every person involved in a relationship has a perception of the relative worth or value of the other. Gary Smalley describes this perception as possessing and expressing a sense of "honor" for one's mate.[7] Do you feel fortunate and blessed to be in relationship with your significant other? Perhaps that feeling can be understood through this analogy: Have you ever dreamed about one day being blessed with a particularly special article of clothing or jewelry or automobile or home? You may feel that it is a bit out of reach, yet one day you happen upon it—and to your surprise, the asking price is just within your ability and far below the normal market value. As you excitedly make the purchase and walk away, in the back of your mind you think, "What a steal!" You are feeling so proud of yourself and can hardly wait to share the news with family and friends. This is the sense of value we should have for our life's mate.

6. THE TEST OF GAIN OR DRAIN (2 CORINTHIANS 6:14 - 18)

Does spending considerable time with this person build me up, leave me neutral, or tear me down? Do I feel as if I am always giving or always getting? Do I leave this person's presence edified or petrified?

One evening a friend of mine who was engaged called me on the phone and sounded a bit irritated. When I asked him what was wrong, he said: "Man, Shaniqua has been over here all day, but she gets on my nerves and she just left a few minutes ago." My response was, "You mean you are about to spend the rest of your *life* with this woman, and you are complaining about three or four *hours?*" Needless to say, they never got married.

After spending time around your prospective lifetime partner, you should feel energized, encouraged, built up, motivated, and inspired. And of course, this feeling should be mutual rather than one-sided. When one partner primarily gives and the other primarily receives, the giving partner will eventually become drained. A drained partner is a dangerous partner. Naturally there will be periods when one partner must give more than the other, but this should not be the norm. The best scenario is when both partners are already fulfilled within themselves and thus are also able to give sufficiently to the other. The result should be a sense of overflow through which both partner's inner resources are constantly being renewed.

7. THE TEST OF COMMITMENT (MATTHEW 19:4 - 6)

Is my partner at the very top of my human priority list, above parents, siblings, friends, former lovers, and possessions? Am I willing without reservation to commit myself wholeheartedly to this person and to wake up next to him or her every morning for the next fifty years?

Commitment is the beefed-up bouncer who works the marriage door of Club Love. Commitment's assignment is to refuse admission to underage wannabes such as Mr. Crush or Miss Infatuation. Commitment also patrols the premises to detect and remove any cleverly disguised perpetrators such as jealousy or lust. Commitment represents a willingness to make the dynamic decision that my partner is more important to me than anyone else. Furthermore, true commitment means saying no to every other past, present, and future relationship in order to say yes to this one. Almost anyone could stay married for six months or a year without much effort. But the real deal is a permanent, lifetime commitment with no emergency escape hatches.

8. THE TEST OF TIME *(ECCLESIASTES 3:1 – 8; LUKE 14:28 – 29)*

This relationship may seem "right" for me, but is it also "ripe" for me?

Are you in a hurry to get married? Do you have a long-distance relationship that has not had the benefit of being up close and personal? Have you dated for more than a year and allowed adequate time for your relationship to develop emotional maturity, situational readiness, and relational ripeness? The presence of two mature people obviously helps to create a mature relationship. But even beyond individual maturity, the relationship must have adequate time to grow and mature on its own. It is foolish to pick a green apple from a tree before it has had time for its sweetness to emerge when ripened by the sun. There is no substitute for timing and process. It takes four seasons to make a year, and a relationship cannot be adequately evaluated on the basis of a summer love alone. Time is our friend. Time will reveal things about our partner and ourselves as nothing else can do. So let us work with time, not against it.

9. THE TEST OF FINANCE *(LUKE 14:28 – 30)*

Have both of us lived within our financial means and handled money well during our life us singles? Are we financially prepared for the expenses involved in marriage?

Have you and your partner jointly designed a budget that reflects outstanding debts and forecasts wedding expenses? Have you considered moving-in costs with enough left over for unforeseen expenses?

Do you tithe? Can you make it on one income in the event a baby arrives or one partner is laid off the job? Do you have adequate health, life, and auto insurance? Do you have a savings account or investments? Do you have a job? I hate to burst any idealistic marriage bubbles, but matrimony can be expensive. Unfortunately, the supermarket does not accept love-tokens at the checkout counter. You must pay to play in this game.

I have watched many young couples marry without their having had the experience of living on their own and paying all their own bills. They nonchalantly wander across the highway of life toward the promised land of matrimony unaware that they can easily get broadsided by the eighteen-wheeler of reality when the bill collectors begin referring to them by their first names and the pressure of debt begins to weaken the infrastructure of their love. One of the foremost contributors to the American divorce rate is that infamous enemy of romance called finance.

10. THE TEST OF CHEMISTRY (PROVERBS 30:18 - 19; SONG OF SONGS)

Do we click? Do I feel physically and emotionally drawn to my partner, and am I pleased by his or her presence and touch? Would I be easily motivated to unselfishly satisfy my partner sexually, and would I still desire nearness even if sex were not on the menu?

This is the fun and relatively easy part. Unfortunately, this step is the only one that some couples take in their decision for marriage. Men and women were designed to be attracted to each other, and fortunately, most of us are not attracted to every single man or woman we meet. There should be something about your life partner that attracts you to him or her more than to any other person. It should not be a temporary mood or a passing fancy but should be a powerful and lasting alliance that links the mind, body, and soul.

11. THE TEST OF GODLY COUNSEL (PROVERBS 11:14)

Have I taken the time to expose my relationship and marriage plans to the caring examination of a trusted and competent counselor?

Some aspects of life can be easily overlooked by a couple who are close. These issues can often be caught by an experienced and unbiased counselor with a godly perspective. Some people, especially men, have a problem with pride when it comes to having a third party intervene to assess the health and welfare of a relationship. However, the same person who disdains seeing a counselor would not hesitate to invite a professional appraiser to inspect a house that's for sale or to seek competent medical advice prior to a major operation. When my wife and I were engaged, we visited no less than four different professional counselors-ministers in order to gain a balanced perspective about our relationship. As a result of the helpful insight we received, we postponed our wedding date twice in order to make some needed repairs. Marriage is a long-distance trip, and it just makes good sense to get your relationship car checked by a professional before beginning your journey.

12. THE TEST OF AGAPE LOVE (1 CORINTHIANS 13)

Am I a selfish person? Would I rather please my partner more than I would like to please myself? Am I willing to do all I can to help my mate reach his or her fullest potential? Do we love each other just as we are without expecting each other to change?

Selfishness is the polar opposite of what it means to be married. The epitome of marriage is a total willingness to share with our partner. Selfishness short-circuits marriage and keeps it from functioning properly. Sometimes when people say, "I love you," what they really mean is, "You meet my needs and make me happy."[8] This self-centered approach is dangerous in that it makes no provision for the inevitable moment when this kind of lover is no longer happy and his or her needs are no longer being met. Selflessness goes against the grain of normal human well-being. The divine element is needed to help love rise from the natural level to the supernatural level. A few of the divine thoughts on love can be found in 1 Corinthians 13:4–8, 13.

In their book *Friends, Lovers, and Soul Mates*, Derek and Darlene Hobson offer this insight:

> When a man sacrifices his individual desire so that his partner can get what she wants, when a woman agrees to forgo her own needs to meet those of her soul mate, each one is saying, "Strengthening this partnership means more to me than having

my way." To renounce personal desires without expectation of reward is to offer love that comes straight from the heart.[9]

Common love is conditional, but agape love is unconditional and is not based on another's performance. Most of what masquerades as love in contemporary culture is a far cry from the original intention of the Inventor. The only way to detect an imitation is to compare it with the genuine. The only source of true love is in God, because God not only *gives* love, but *is* love. Perhaps this perspective is best summarized in Jawanza Kunjufu's book *The Power, Passion and Pain of Black Love:*

> As you work on your relationship with the Lord, as you become more and more like Him, as you begin to love Him the way He loves you, love begins to exude out of you. If your mate can also love the Lord the way the Lord loves you, you will find that you have God loving God. You will have God's love coming out of you and God's love coming out of your mate and oh hallelujah when you have God loving God![10]

LET'S TALK!

1. Do you think that the high American divorce rate is related more to a mismatch in initial mate choice or to an unwillingness to work on differences?

2. If you were engaged, what amount of counseling would you be willing to submit to?

   A. None
   B. One session
   C. Three to four sessions
   D. Eight to ten sessions
   E. Unlimited—whatever it takes

3. Would you be willing to change your wedding plans in terms of timing, financial preparation, or other ways if the counseling indicated it would be wise to do so?

4. Would you be willing to terminate the relationship if this recommendation emerged from the counseling?
5. Do you think that sexually active couples would be willing to refrain from sex until marriage if this issue arose during counseling?
6. Which of the twelve steps do you find most helpful for determining your life's mate or assessing your current relationship? Can you think of additional steps that merit consideration?
7. Be sure to read each of the Scripture references related to the twelve tests. In what ways do they help to clarify each test?

Chapter 12

WHO'S LOVING YOU?

Ingredients in Intimacy and Lessons in Love

When I was in junior high school, the musical group The Jackson Five was all the rage. James Brown was also burning up the charts, but the Jacksons were our age. We even had a student group that could cover their songs. One song that made all the girls scream was "Who's Loving You?" In this song the man confesses that when they were together, "I treated you baaaaaad." But now that she's gone, he just sits around with his head hanging down while wondering "who's loving you?" One might argue that this ex-"lover" should have spent his time in more constructive activities than those just described. Perhaps he could have conducted a personal inventory to discover the causes of his own shortcomings while making the personal alterations necessary to prevent such relationship errors in the future. But this is not about relational psychoanalysis—it's just a love song. It simply poses a basic question that I would like to borrow and pose to you: "Who's loving *you?*"

Your honest answer and awareness of this question will greatly determine how you feel about yourself and how much love you are able to extend to others. Three components are crucial to completing this love connection. In many ways this chapter is a summary of several important points previously stated in this book.

IS FAMILY LOVING ME?

Recent research confirms the fact that a child's initial lessons about love are learned in the home. This is true whether those lessons are harmful or helpful. Barbara De Angelis offers an excellent equation for understanding the effect of the home environment on our love choices and perceptions:

If A=B, and B=C, then A=C

If love=home, and home=chaos, then love=chaos

If love=home, and home=loneliness, then love=loneliness

If love=home, and home=fear, then love=fear[1]

The De Angelis premise is clear: Our minds equate home associations with love associations. Depending on whether home was good, bad, or average, we look for a love that is good, bad, or average. However, a bad childhood need not doom us to a lifetime of bad love. Regardless of its power, any family curse can and must be reversed. A victim need not become a victimizer.

ARE YOU LOVING YOU?

You've heard it a thousand times: You've got to love yourself. You may say that you already love yourself. If that is true, you will be able to easily answer this question: "In what specific ways do you love yourself?" Why not take some time right now and make a list? If you cannot think of ways you already intentionally express love to yourself, write down some ways that you would like to express it. Life becomes tragic when we need someone else around us in order to truly enjoy ourselves. It is said that to be bored is an insult to oneself because it indicates an inability or lack of creativity in making something interesting happen without outside help.

IS GOD LOVING YOU?

Although we may theoretically embrace the idea that God loves us, for most people this love is of a very generic nature. Most people understand a God who expresses love for everybody, everywhere, all the time. This concept is accurate, but it is also incomplete. As long as we embrace a generic level of God's love, the quality of our relationship with God will always have a generic quality. God desires to have a personal, intimate designer relationship with us. It is an awesome thought to realize that the Creator of the universe desires to forge an intimate bond with us. When we move from a detached, abstract view of God to a unique, personal friendship, as expressed in the Bible, this will mark our spiritual turning point and our entire existence will blossom (John 10:10).

God's love, self-love, and family love are essential for sane living. At the very least, we must have the first two. After that, anything else is a bonus. Even if we can only sense God's love, we are still in a good position to progress in life.

Much of our success in life depends on understanding and acting upon our life's purpose. Why were you created? Can you fulfill your purpose as a single person? Author-minister Myles Munroe contends, "We have confused singleness with being alone!" He illustrates this idea with a key ring: "Each key is unique, separate, and whole, yet all of the keys are joined by a common ring. The keys are single, but not alone; thus it is possible to be single but not alone."[2]

The primary purpose of a woman is not to fulfill a man, and vice versa. The general purpose of any person is—

1. To know, love, and obey God.
2. To know, love, and fulfill self.
3. To know, love, and serve others.

When purpose is in perspective, life takes on a balance that is not hindered by adverse circumstances. When I am filled up, I can generously give back. But when my inner resources become depleted, my fountain of intimacy runs dry.

Our intimacy with others takes four shapes: emotional, intellectual, spiritual, and physical. Some of these are more significant than others, depending on the people involved, the progress of their relationship, and their positions in life. However, it would be a mistake, for example, to substitute spiritual intimacy with physical intimacy or to maximize the intellectual and minimize the emotional. Each aspect has its own pace and place. Balance is the key.

RELATIONSHIP HOUSE

If you had to compare a past or current relationship to a building, what kind of building would it be: A trailer? A tent? A split-level condominium? A skyscraper? Use your imagination. The possibilities are endless. In my seminars I sometimes ask groups to construct their ideal relationship house and to identify the primary parts: the foundation, the walls, the roof, and so forth. The results are usually very interesting and creative. As stated in chapter 4, the most important aspect of a relationship is also the least visible: the foundation. What is your foundation? Is it trust, communication, honesty, friendship, a good sex life? Although all these are important and valuable, not one of them is durable enough to serve as the foundation. Such an important element of the house requires something strong, solid, and changeless. These are characteristics that only God can provide. When we choose God as our foundation, the rest of the house sits on a stable source of support (Matthew 6:33).

LOVE

I have a problem with the words we use to express our concept of love. You can call it semantics, or just nit-picking, but I question why people say, "I'm falling in love" and "I want to make love to you." First, I'm not so sure I want to fall into anything. That sounds like an accident. Allow me to suggest that love is more like a climb than a fall. Falls are dangerous and damaging; climbs offer energetic exercise, enhanced views, and accomplished goals. Then there is the term "making love," which usually refers to sexual intercourse. To make something implies that the process creates the result. However, the act of sexual intercourse does not create or produce love; rather, it is designed to strengthen and enhance the love that should already exist.

Some of the contemporary nomenclature for love does seem appropriate. Take "puppy love," for example. As with newborn pups, "puppy love" is blind and unable to discern its surroundings realistically due to its infatuation. Puppy love sometimes changes into full-grown canine love. The problem is that, even though it has matured some, it is still quite capable of "dogging" its partner.

Dr. Kermit T. Mehlinger describes healthy, mature love this way:

> Mature love is distinguished by reciprocation. I like to think of it as a duet, and of infatuation as a solo in which one individual falls in love with a fantasy of his [or her] own making. Mature love is dynamic. It grows and it sees the beloved as a real person with faults as well as virtues.[3]

The English language is somewhat limited in its ability to describe love. Classical Greek exercised more latitude and variety in its conceptualizations through offering several different words that we translate as *love:*

> *Storge* refers to the cherishing of blood relatives; especially parents and children.
> *Philautos/phileo* refers to the fondness found in friendship.
> *Eros* refers to the erotic, to sexual love.
> *Agapao/Agape* refers to affectionate benevolence—a deliberate act of the will to express unconditional favor toward another.[4]

This variety of definitions enables a clear and more specific understanding as to which way a particular love relationship may be leaning. Under the best conditions, it is obvious that the strongest and most versatile level of love would contain a combination of all four kinds.

Many of the concepts and perspectives in this book have been presented in formula style with steps and lists. This was done because segmenting a complicated concept is often the most efficient approach to understanding and demystifying it. Having said that, I must in all honesty say this as well: Life will not always follow such perfectly prescribed steps. No single life will always fit into every formula. You can follow relationship rules with matchless perfection and individual results may vary. You may gracefully glide through every step in the staircase of singleness and still stumble at the top of the landing. Life is not like a playbook, but more like a journal. It is obviously a wise thing to know the script in this drama called life, but it is also quite helpful to be spontaneous when necessary. Your ability to climb life's mountain depends on your agility and ability to overcome life's obstacles.

As a single, the apostle Paul set a great example of a positive, progressive attitude. Herein lies the secret of success in life:

> I have learned to be content whatever the circumstances. I know what it is to be in need, and I know what it is to have plenty. I have learned the secret of being content in any and every situation, whether well fed or hungry, whether living in plenty or in want. I can do everything through [Christ] who gives me strength (Philippians 4:11–13).

We are called to express our best and trust God for the rest. When we creatively incorporate God's power into our lives we can count on a future filled with favor as expressed in Jeremiah 29:11: "'For I know the plans that I have for you,' declares the LORD, 'plans to prosper you and not to harm you, plans to give you hope and a future.'"

LET'S TALK!

1. In what ways is the word *love* typically misunderstood and misused?
2. Why are some people so reluctant to use the "L" word?
3. How is one able to become more comfortable with verbally expressing one's love?
4. Is it necessary to verbally express one's love to one's loved one?
5. Is it possible for love to die?
6. How is human love different from God's love?
7. How can we become fit so that God can love others through us?
8. Re-read 1 Corinthians 13 and make a list of love's primary characteristics. Which of these do you usually express and in which areas do you need to grow?

MORE CREATIVE CONVERSATION

The following list augments the suggestions found in chapter 5. As with that listing, some of the following work well with new dating partners and some are better left to a more mature relationship. You are the best judge of what is appropriate and when.

BONUS CATEGORY: EXCEPTIONAL ETCETERAS

1. What are your strongest likes and dislikes?
2. What do you feel are the three most momentous events in history?
3. Describe your dream job.
4. What sport do you or would you love to play?
5. Do you have an artistic side?
6. What is your concept of proper gender roles?
7. What are your best and worst habits?
8. What are your hobbies (past, present, and future)?
9. What qualities build a great relationship?
10. What are your personal talents?
11. What is your most important material possession?
12. How do you feel about interracial relationships and marriage?
13. How do you visualize the future of the world?
14. In what ways do you use your imagination?

15. What is your view of politics and government?
16. What site would you like most to visit in national or international travel?
17. What is the world's greatest problem? Asset?
18. What is your greatest problem? Asset?
19. What is my greatest problem? Asset?
20. What is the most beautiful natural creation to you?
21. Who are your mentors?
22. What are your thoughts about death?
23. What is your idea of great entertainment?
24. What is the best advice you have ever been given?
25. In what ways are you disciplined and undisciplined?
26. What social graces do you have and do you need?
27. In what ways do you demonstrate kindness?
28. What is your greatest hindrance to communication?
29. Which of the following traits do you have most and need most: love, joy, peace, patience, gentleness, goodness, faith, or humility?
30. What is your favorite outfit to wear?
31. What is your favorite outfit for me to wear?
32. What is your favorite subject to discuss?
33. What topic are you most comfortable with discussing?
34. If you could ask God one question, what would it be?
35. Ask me anything you wish.
36. What advice did your parents give you about relationships?
37. Describe your early relationship with your father and your present relationship with him.
38. Are there issues between you and family members that are still unresolved?
39. If you could relive your family life, what things would you do similarly, and what would you do differently?
40. Who is the "power person" or opinion-shaper within your family?
41. What are your earliest memories of references to God?
42. What is your current relationship with God, and how did that come about?

43. What part does God play in your everyday decision making?
44. What are your feelings about various religions and denominations?
45. How do you feel about attending church? What about active membership?
46. What is your purpose in life? Do you have a personal ministry?
47. If you died today, do you think God would be pleased or displeased with your life?
48. What was/is your high school or college grade-point average?
49. Do you plan to continue your education at some point? If so, what do you want to study?
50. Give an example of what you consider to be common sense.
51. What were your strongest and weakest subjects in school?
52. What subject matter always piques your interest and curiosity?
53. What kinds of people are you most comfortable around?
54. Imagine you have a totally free day. How will you spend it?
55. Do you want a large family or a small family?
56. Rank the following in order of importance: friends, parents, siblings, spouse, employer.
57. What person or persons have had the greatest impact on your life?
58. How often do you get physical checkups?
59 Do you have a savings account or invest in a mutual fund?
60. How many credit cards do you have, and what are the balances?
61. Do you spend more than you keep?
62. What do you expect to teach, learn, gain, or accomplish through a dating relationship?
63. Have you ever lied to me?

NOTES

Chapter 1. Singleness: Burden, Blessing, or Both?

1. Robyn Gool, *For Singles Only* (Tulsa: Christian Publishing Services, 1987), 12.

2. Joni Eareckson Tada, personal statement.

3. Robert G. Allen, *No Money Down for the 90's* (New York: Simon & Schuster, 1990), 142–43.

4. John Avanzini, *The Debt Term–O–Nator* (Fort Worth, TX: His Publishing Co., 1993), 33.

Chapter 2. Male and Female: Appreciating the Differences

1. *Webster's New Riverside University Dictionary* (Boston: Houghton Mifflin, 1984).

2. Gary R. Brooks, *The Centerfold Syndrome* (New York: Jossey Bass, 1995).

3. Gary Smalley, *Making Love Last Forever* (Dallas: Word Publishing, 1996), 21–26.

4. John Gray, *Men Are from Mars, Women Are from Venus* (New York: Harper Collins, 1992), 29–33.

5. Ibid.

6. Cornel West, *Race Matters* (New York: Vintage Books, 1993), 119.

7. Smalley, *Making Love Last Forever*, 24.

8. Bebe Moore Campbell, "Halle Berry, The Inside Story," *Essence*, October 1996, 70.

9. Alvis O. Davis, *Black Men Not Looking for Sex: Why They Commit Forever* (San Jose, CA: Zevon Publications, 1995).

10. Ibid., 24.

11. Ibid., 25.

12. Ibid.

Chapter 3. No Condom for the Mind

1. Bonnie Pfister, "Swept Awake," *The Progressive Women's Quarterly* (Spring 1994), 14.

2. Toby Simon, "Sexuality on Campus—90's Style," *Change* (September–October 1993), 50–57.

3. Larry Trotter, *Gospel Today* (February 1998), 44–45.

4. Robert T. Michael et al., *Sex in America: A Definitive Study* (New York: Warner Books, 1994), 93–94.

5. Mary D. Pellauer, "A Modest Amount of Sex," *Christian Century* (June 1995), 21–28.

6. Pfister, "Swept Awake," 14.

7. Patricia Funderburk Ware, "An Open Letter to the African-American

Churches." Ware is director of Educational Services for Americans for a Sound AIDS/HIV Policy, P.O. Box 17433, Washington, DC 20041.

8. Study cited by Funderburk.

9. Simon, "Sexuality on Campus—90's Style," 50.

10. Ibid.

11. Ibid.

12. Pfister, "Swept Awake," 13.

13. Jan Farrington, "Sex and Responsibility: What does the 'R' word mean to you?" *Current Health* (September 1995), 12.

14. Rick Stedman, *Pure Joy! The Positive Side of Single Sexuality* (Chicago: Moody Press, 1993), 77.

15. Ibid., 98.

Chapter 4. Sanctified Sex

1. See *Strong's Exhaustive Concordance* (Nashville: Thomas Nelson, 1990), 876.

2. See Myles Munroe, "Purpose," audiocassette series, Bahama Faith Ministries International, P.O. Box N-9583, Nassau, The Bahamas.

3. Marva J. Dawn, *Sexual Character* (Grand Rapids: Eerdmans, 1993), 18.

4. Janie Gustafson, "Celibate Passion," *Sexuality and the Sacred* (Louisville: Westminster/John Knox Press, 1994), 277.

5. Dawn, *Sexual Character*, 12.

6. Ibid., 10.

7. Ray Mossholder, *Singles Plus* (Lake, Mary, FL: Creation House, 1991).

8. "Why Some People Consider Celibacy," *Jet* (December 22, 1997), 14.

9. Ibid., 12.

10. Rick Stedman, *Pure Joy! The Positive Side of Single Sexuality* (Chicago: Moody Press, 1993), 151.

11. John White, *Eros Redeemed* (Downers Grove, IL: InterVarsity Press, 1993), 215.

12. T. D. Jakes, "Admit It, Quit It, Forget It," videotape VT0200 from T. D. Jakes Ministries, P.O. Box 5390, Dallas, TX 75208.

Chapter 6. Common Questions, Uncommon Answers

1. Three large Black Christian Singles Conferences include: (1) The Missouri-Black Christian Single Adult Retreat. Meets each June in Roach, MO at beautiful retreat area. Contact Missouri Baptist Convention (573)635-7931, ext. 511. (2) The National Black Christian Singles Conference. Meets each October at various locations in Texas. Sponsored by Brentwood Baptist Church. Contact Rev. John Holman (713) 729-5933 ext. 39. (3) T. D. James Ministries Singles Conference. Meets each September in various locations. Call 1-800-2474672.

2. Ray Short, *Sex, Love, or Infatuation: Can I Really Know?* (Minneapolis: Augsburg, 1990).

3. Sheron C. Patterson, *Single Principles* (Dallas: Perseverance Press, 1993), 60.

4. This insight was gleaned from a conversation with a single friend, Avery L. Blakeney.

Chapter 7. Solo Sex

1. Barry St. Clair and Bill Jones, *Sex: Desiring the Best* (San Bernardino, CA: Here's Life, 1987), 115.

2. Robert T. Michael et al., *Sex in America: A Definitive Study* (New York: Warner Books, 1994), 166.

3. Ibid.

4. Ibid., 167.

5. Ibid., 160.

6. Ibid., 161.

7. Leland Elliot and Cynthia Brantley, *Sex on Campus* (New York: Random House, 1997), 102.

8. Michael et al., *Sex in America*, 162.

9. Randy Alcorn, *Christians in the Wake of the Sexual Revolution* (Portland, OR: Multnomah Press, 1985), 215.

10. St. Clair and Jones, *Sex: Desiring the Best*, 115.

11. Greg Speck, *Sex: It's Worth Waiting For* (Chicago: Moody Press, 1989), 149.

12. John White, *Eros Defiled* (Downers Grove, IL: InterVarsity Press, 1977), 43.

13. Ray Short, *Sex, Dating and Love* (Minneapolis: Augsburg, 1984), 117.

14. Jim Burns, *Handling Your Hormones: The "Straight Scoop" on Love and Sexuality* (Eugene, OR: Harvest House, 1986), 109.

15. Rick Stedman, *Pure Joy! The Positive Side of Single Sexuality* (Chicago: Moody Press, 1993), 203.

16. Ibid., 201.

Chapter 8. Date Rape

1. Robert T. Michael et al., *Sex in America: A Definitive Study* (New York: Warner Books, 1994), 166.

2. Ibid., 225.

3. Leland Elliot and Cynthia Brantley, *Sex on Campus* (New York: Random House, 1997).

4. Betty Wagner, "Struggling with Sex," *U.S. News & World Report*, 26 September 1994, 117.

Chapter 9. Homosexuality

1. Robert T. Michael et al., *Sex in America: A Definitive Study* (New York: Warner Books, 1994), 176.

2. Herant A. Katchadourian and Donald T. Lunde, *Fundamentals of Human Sexuality* (New York: Holt, Rinehart and Winston, 1972), 265.

3. Greg Speck, *Sex: It's Worth Waiting For* (Chicago: Moody Press, 1989), 176.

4. Michael et al., *Sex in America*, 172.

5. John White, *Eros Defiled* (Downers Grove, IL: InterVarsity Press, 1977), 117.

6. The author is grateful to Santoria Alsup for his professional insight, perspective, and clarification with regard to this chapter's subject matter.

7. White, *Eros Defiled*, 119.

8. Leland Elliot and Cynthia Brantley, *Sex on Campus* (New York: Random House, 1997), 17.

9. Betty Berzon, *The Intimacy Dance* (New York: Penguin Books, 1996), 149.

Chapter 10. Breaking Up Without Breaking Down

1. Mira Kirshenbaum, *Too Good to Leave, Too Bad to Stay* (New York: Dutton, 1996), 207.

2. Ibido, 25.

Chapter 11. How to Recognize Mr. or Ms. Right

1. *New Man*, March–April 1997. For a fuller explanation of a Community Marriage Policy, see Michael McManus, *Marriage Savers: Helping Your Friends and Family Stay Married* (Grand Rapids: Zondervan, 1993).

2. See M. Blaine Smith, *Should I Get Married?* (Downers Grove, IL: InterVarsity Press, 1990), 80–86.

3. Ibid., 15ff.

4. Barbara De Angelis, *Are You the One for Me?* (New York: Dell Books, 1992), 117.

5. Juanita Bynahm "No More Sheets" video T. D. Jakes Ministries, P.O. Box 5390, Dallas, Texas 75208.

6. Jo Lynn Pool, *A Good Man Is Hard to Find* (Nashville: Thomas Nelson, 1995).

7. Gary Smalley, *Making Love Last Forever* (Dallas: Word Books, 1996), 135.

8. Jim Conway, *Men in Mid-Life Crisis* (Elgin, IL: David C. Cook, 1978), 187.

9. Derek S. Hobson and Darlene Powell Hobson, *Friends, Loves, and Soul Mates* (New York: Simon & Schuster, 1994), 51.

10. Jawanza Kunjufu, *The Power, Passion and Pain of Black Love* (Chicago: African American Images, 1993), 153.

Chapter 12. Who's Loving You?

1. Barbara De Angelis, *Are You the One for Me?* (New York: Dell Books, 1992), 66.

2. Myles Munroe, *Single, Married, Separated, and Life After Divorce* (Shippensburg, PA: Destiny Image Publishers, 1992), 15.

3. Dr. Kermit H. Mehlinger, personal quotation.

4. See *Strong's Exhaustive Concordance* (Nashville: Thomas Nelson, 1990).

These exciting seminars by Chris Jackson are just some of those available for presentation at your church, campus, or convention:

- The Black Christian Singles Guide to Dating and Sexuality
- Establishing an Effective Ministry with Black College Students
- Creative Approaches to Teaching: Avoiding the Sin of Boring People with the Bible
- Gospel Choir or a Choir That Sings Gospel? Understanding Music as Ministry
- Diversity Without Adversity: Examining the Race Issue Without Grudge or Guilt
- The Power of Purpose: Discovering Our Spiritual Gifts
- The Holy Spirit: Divinely Programmed or Humanly Practiced?
- A Scriptural Perspective on Women in Ministry

(All seminars are interactive and are available with audio/video technical support.)

For information and scheduling, contact Chris Jackson at
Creative Ministry Concepts
Suite 601 Cavendish Court
Nashville, Tennessee 37013–2849
Phone and fax: (615) 399–0883
E-mail: CreateNMe@aol.com

Visit our Web page at
www.MinistryConcepts.com

We want to hear from you. Please send your comments about this book to us in care of the address below. Thank you.

GRAND RAPIDS, MICHIGAN 49530

www.zondervan.com